CONTENTS

Bangkok Area by Area

Old City.................................**68**

Chinatown.............................**76**

Downtown...............................**84**

Greater Bangkok.....................**94**

Beyond Bangkok.....................**102**

Streetsmart

Getting To and Around Bangkok.................................**108**

Practical Information................**110**

Places to Stay...........................**114**

General Index............................**118**

Acknowledgments......................**124**

Phrase Book...............................**126**

Within each Top 10 list in this book, no hierarchy of quality or popularity is implied. All 10 are, in the editor's opinion, of roughly equal merit.

Throughout this book, floors are referred to in accordance with American usage; i.e., the "first floor" is at ground level.

Title page, front cover and spine *The stunning Wat Arun at sunset*
Back cover, clockwise from top left *Damnoen Saduak Floating Market; Bangkok cityscape; Chinatown; Wat Arun; Wat Benjamabophit*

Welcome to
Bangkok

A study in contrasts, Bangkok is simultaneously traditional and modern, noisy and serene. Outside even the glitziest Western-style building, you'll find a small but well-tended shrine respecting the spirit of the land. A city of surprises, it's held together by the famed hospitality of the Thai people. With Eyewitness Top 10 Bangkok, it's yours to explore.

The massive **Chao Phraya River** bisects Bangkok as it flows into the nearby Gulf of Thailand. Along its eastern bank lies the **Old City**, centered around **Rattanakosin**, Bangkok's royal heart, with its spectacular **Grand Palace**, the gleaming treasures of the **National Museum**, and a number of Buddhist temples.

Just downstream lie **Chinatown**'s markets, gold shops, and Taoist shrines. Bangkokians have embraced their riverside roots, and many art galleries and hip pubs take advantage of the low-rise buildings on the river and cool breezes. Inland, you'll find ultramodern downtown hotels, restaurants, and shops, especially among the glass skyscrapers in Silom. Across the river, in **Thonburi**, the unique Khmer-style temple of **Wat Arun** and quiet canals offer a glimpse of a life that could not be more different from the one just over the water.

Whether you're visiting for a weekend or a week, our Top 10 guide brings together the best of everything the city has to offer, from the temples and museums of the Old City to the nightlife Downtown. The guide has useful tips throughout, from seeking what's free to avoiding the crowds, plus seven easy-to-follow itineraries, designed to tie together a clutch of sights in a short space of time. Add inspiring photography and detailed maps, and you've got the essential pocket-sized travel companion. **Enjoy the book, and enjoy Bangkok**.

Clockwise from top: Giant feet of a Buddha image at Wat Indrawiharn, a boat filled with hats in Damnoen Saduak Floating Market, traffic on Yaowarat Road in Chinatown, lakeside pavilion at Muang Boran, Buddha statues at Wat Pho, the Emerald Green Pagoda at Wat Pak Nam, near Khlong Bangkok Yai, a cannonball flower

Exploring Bangkok

Although Bangkok is huge, many of its sights are within walking distance of each other along the river or in nearby Downtown. Using a combination of river boats and mass transit, it's largely possible to avoid the notorious traffic jams. Here are our suggestions for the best things to experience in either two or four days.

Rattanakosin art from the 18th to 20th centuries can be admired in the National Museum.

Wat Phra Kaeo is a complex of prayer halls, towers, and *chedis* (stupas) within the grounds of the Grand Palace.

Two Days in Bangkok

Day ❶

MORNING

Start off with a visit to the magnificent **Wat Phra Kaeo** (see pp12–13) and the adjacent **Grand Palace** (see pp14–15), taking time for the excellent Queen Sirikit Museum of Textiles. Walk down to the Chao Phraya River and have lunch at one of the small restaurants at **Tha Maharaj** (see p73).

AFTERNOON

After lunch, stroll the grounds of **Wat Pho** (see pp18–19) and enjoy a back rub in the temple's massage school. Next, visit the **National Museum** (see pp16–17). Have dinner at the **Blue Elephant** restaurant (see p99), then board the boat from Tha Saphan Taksin to Asiatique the Riverfront and take in the **Calypso Cabaret** (see p101).

Day ❷

MORNING

Take a water taxi to **Wat Arun** (see pp30–31), on the Thonburi side of the river, then hop on the Saen Saeb canal boat to **Jim Thompson House** (see pp28–9), the home of the American who revived the Thai silk industry.

AFTERNOON

Browse the **shopping malls** (see p89) on Rama I Road, then take in the Thai dance show at **Siam Niramit** (see p101).

Four Days in Bangkok

Day ❶

MORNING

Cross the river to Thonburi to visit the stunning "Temple of Dawn",

Damnoen Saduak Floating Market is renowned for its noodle sellers, who prepare delicious traditional dishes inside *sampan* (rowing boats) on the canal.

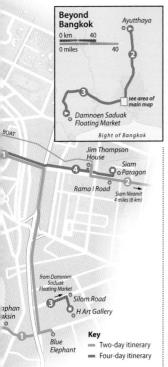

Beyond Bangkok

0 km   40

0 miles   40

Ayutthaya

see area of main map

Damnoen Saduak Floating Market

Bight of Bangkok

Jim Thompson House

Siam Paragon

Rama I Road

Siam Niramit
4 miles (6 km)

from Damnoen Saduak Floating Market

Silom Road

H Art Gallery

aphan aksin

Blue Elephant

Key

— Two-day itinerary

— Four-day itinerary

bicycle or hire a tuk-tuk to visit the many temples and museums.

AFTERNOON

Indulge yourself with a treatment at one of Bangkok's many excellent **spas** *(see pp46–7)*, then take in the sunset from **Tha Maharaj** *(see p73)*.

Day ❸

MORNING

Wake early to visit the **Damnoen Saduak Floating Market** *(see pp24–5)*.

AFTERNOON

Enjoy the contemporary artworks on display at the **H Gallery** on Silom Road *(see p42)*.

Day ❹

MORNING

Head to **Wat Pho** *(see pp18–19)*, admire the huge **Reclining Buddha**, and spare some time afterwards for a traditional massage on the temple grounds.

AFTERNOON

Visit **Jim Thompson House** *(see pp28–9)*, followed by a shopping trip to nearby **Siam Paragon** *(see p89)* and the other malls on Rama I Road.

Jim Thompson House, a delightful treasure trove of the most exquisite Southeast Asian antiques and art.

Wat Arun *(see pp30–31)*, and the **Royal Barge Museum** *(see p96)*.

AFTERNOON

Visit the **Wat Phra Kaeo** *(see pp12–13)*, **Grand Palace** *(see pp14–15)*, and the **National Museum** *(see pp16–17)*. Dine on the river *(see p90)*, then listen to some jazz at **Brown Sugar: The Jazz Boutique** *(see p74)*.

Day ❷

MORNING

Visit the ancient Siamese capital of **Ayutthaya** *(see pp32–5)*. Rent a

Top 10 Bangkok Highlights

Buddha statues under a colonnade
at the temple of Wat Arun

Grand Palace 12

Wat Phra Kaeo 14

National Museum 16

Wat Pho 18

Bangkok's Canals 20

Damnoen Saduak
Floating Market 24

Chatuchak Weekend Market 26

Jim Thompson House 28

Wat Arun 30

Ayutthaya 32

🔟 Bangkok Highlights

Beguiling and bewildering, spiritual and sensual, Bangkok is one of Asia's most intriguing cities. Its glittering temples and museums overflow with art, while the city's canals and markets reveal the locals' friendly nature. Shopping, dining out, and reveling in the vibrant nightlife should feature high on everyone's itinerary.

Wat Phra Kaeo ①

A fabulous patchwork of colors and shapes, the Wat Phra Kaeo temple is Thailand's holiest site, and is the pinnacle of perfection in Thai religious art and architecture *(see pp12–13).*

② Grand Palace

A dazzling complex comprising a number of historic buildings, pavilions, courtyards and gardens. An unmissable sight *(see pp14–15).*

③ National Museum

One of the largest museums in Asia, it has priceless exhibits including intricate works of art that document the long and eventful history of Thailand *(see pp16–17).*

④ Wat Pho

Bangkok's oldest and biggest temple, and formerly a center for public education, Wat Pho houses a massive Reclining Buddha and a school of Thai massage *(see pp18–19).*

Bangkok's Canals ⑤

Boats were once the city's main mode of transport. Tour the canals to glimpse a vanishing lifestyle *(see pp20–21).*

6 Damnoen Saduak Floating Market

Though designed for tourists, the colorful sights, aromatic smells, and cheerful banter of vendors make a visit to this floating market a delightful experience (see pp24–5).

7 Chatuchak Weekend Market

Bangkok's biggest market offers the chance to pick up a unique souvenir and feel the pulse of Thai culture in the maze of stalls (see pp26–7).

8 Jim Thompson House

This complex is a fine example of Thai teak architecture. The main house remains as it was in the days of Jim Thompson, the man who made Thai silk world-famous (see pp28–9).

9 Wat Arun

With its five distinctive *prangs* (towers), which are often used as a logo of the city, this temple played an important historical role in the development of Bangkok and remains one of its most attractive sights (see pp30–31).

10 Ayutthaya

The ancient city of Ayutthaya is easily visited in a day. Its huge, crumbling *chedis* (stupas) and blissful Buddha images give an idea of the splendor of this former capital (see pp32–5).

TOP 10 ⭐ Wat Phra Kaeo

The spectacular Wat Phra Kaeo is Thailand's holiest temple, and lies inside of the Grand Palace complex *(see pp14–15)*. It serves as home to the national talisman, the Emerald Buddha, and as the royal chapel of the Grand Palace. There are no resident monks here, and the lavish assemblage is kept in pristine condition. Heavily ornamented statues of mythical creatures called *yakshas* (giants), from Thai legends, stand at the entrance gates, acting as guardians of the temple. It is a stunning display of Thailand's artistic and architectural finesse, and a truly memorable sight.

1 Ramakien Murals
Stretching over half a mile (1 km) along the temple's cloister walls, the *Ramakien* murals **(above)** portray scenes from the Hindu epic *Ramayana* in 178 panels of intricate detail and vibrant color.

2 Phra Mondop
This repository for sacred Buddhist texts is on the upper terrace. Its deep-green mosaics are a perfect backdrop for the seated stone Buddhas in each corner.

3 Phra Si Rattana Chedi
This glittering *chedi* (stupa) is shaped like a cone, and stands majestically on the upper terrace beside the Phra Mondop. It is built of gold tiles in the Sri Lankan style.

4 Royal Pantheon
The pantheon **(left)**, one of a trio of tall buildings on the upper terrace, dates back to the reign of Rama IV. It enshrines life-sized statues of the past rulers of the Chakri dynasty *(see p38)*.

5 Model of Angkor Wat
Tucked away behind the Phra Mondop, this scale model of Angkor Wat was commissioned by Rama IV *(see p38)*, when Cambodia was under Siamese rule.

6 Wihan Yot
Also known as "the porcelain *wihan*", this delicately adorned prayer hall stands to the north of Phra Mondop. It contains a number of Buddha images, including the Nak buddha rescued from Ayutthaya.

7 The Emerald Buddha

Carved out of single piece of jadeite rather than emerald, the most sacred image **(left)** in the kingdom is just 26 in (66 cm) tall. Thought to have been crafted in Sri Lanka, it was housed in Chiang Rai, Lampang, and Laos before Rama I brought it to Bangkok.

MYTHICAL CREATURES IN THAI TEMPLES

A panoply of fearsome creatures guard the entrances to most Thai temple compounds. These are from the legendary forest of Himaphan, a kind of Buddhist Shangri-La up in the Himalayan Mountains. These include *singha*, a lion-like figure, *yaksha*, a giant, *naga*, a serpent-like protector of Buddha, *hongsa*, a swan-like entity, and several other hybrids that are part-man and part-beast.

Temple of the Jewel containing Lord Buddha

8 The Bot

The most visited building in the grounds is the *bot* (ordination hall), which contains the much-venerated Emerald Buddha. Inside, the walls are adorned with murals, and the scent of incense is over-whelming as Thais pay respect to the image that is revered as the country's talisman.

9 Hor Phra Nak and Hor Phra Monthien Tham

Flanking the Wihan Yot are the Hor Phra Nak, a royal mausoleum with urns that hold the ashes of members of the royal family, and the Hor Phra Monthien Tham, a library that has particularly fine doors inlaid with mother-of-pearl.

10 Chapel of Gandahara Buddha

In the southeast corner of the temple compound stands a small chapel with beautifully painted doors. Usually locked, it contains an image, used in the Royal Ploughing Ceremony (see p64), of the Buddha calling down the rains.

NEED TO KNOW

MAP B4 ▪ Na Phra Lan Road ▪ Chao Phraya express boat to Tha Chang ▪ www.royalgrandpalace.th/en

Open 8:30am–3:30pm daily

Adm B500, including Grand Palace (see pp14-15)

▪ Dress modestly. Before entering the premises, make sure you are not wearing sandals, shorts, short skirts, torn or tight trousers, sleeveless, or see-through shirts.

▪ The ticket office is outside the western wall of Wat Phra Kaeo, near the temple's entrance.

TOP 10 ⭐ Grand Palace

In 1782, King Rama I (r.1782–1809) established Bangkok as Siam's capital and built Wat Phra Kaeo *(see pp12–13)* to house the most precious Buddha image in the country. In 1784, he had the adjacent Grand Palace complex built, which became the home of the royal family. Its structure was significantly enhanced by later rulers. No king has resided here since the early 20th century, but the palace's several buildings, ceremonial halls, pavilions, and gardens display a fantastic fusion of Thai and Western aesthetic.

1 Dusit Throne Hall
For many, this building **(left)** is the site's crowning glory, featuring a four-tiered roof and Rama I's teak throne.

2 Amarin Winichai Hall
This building was originally used as an audience hall for foreign guests. Inside, the hall has colorful murals and Rama I's boat-shaped Busabok Mala Throne surmounted by a nine-tiered white canopy. Today, the hall is used for state ceremonies and is open to the public on weekdays.

3 Inner Palace
Until the time of Rama VII (r.1925–35), the Inner Palace was inhabited solely by women. All males except the king were forbidden entry. Still closed to the public, it is now a school for girls from prominent families.

4 Chakri Maha Prasat
Occupying center stage in the Grand Palace is the Chakri throne hall **(below)**. Built in 1882 by Rama V (r.1868–1910), it fuses Western and Thai architecture. The ashes of Chakri kings are housed here.

NEED TO KNOW
MAP B4 ■ Na Phra Lan Road ■ Chao Phraya express boat to Tha Chang ■ www.royal grandpalace.th/en

Open 8:30am–3:30pm daily

Adm B500, including Wat Phra Kaeo *(see pp12–13)* and the Queen Sirikit Museum of Textiles

Queen Sirikit Museum of Textiles: 9am–4:30pm daily (last entry 3:30pm); adm B150 (museum only)

■ Dress modestly; no sandals, shorts, short skirts, torn or tight trousers, sleeveless shirts, crop tops or see-through tops.

■ Carry water, as the only café is at the end of the tour, next to the Dusit Throne Hall.

5 Model of Mount Krailas

Behind the Dusit Throne Hall is an ornamented model of Mount Krailas, thought to be the central mountain of the universe in Hindu and Buddhist mythology. In olden times, royal children would have their topknot cut off here, in an elaborate ceremony to welcome adolescence.

7 Aphonphimok Pavilion

This small but attractive wooden pavilion **(right)** was built by Rama IV (r.1851–68) as a royal changing room prior to giving audiences in the adjacent Dusit Throne Hall. Its multi-tiered roof and gold decoration are hallmarks of traditional Thai architecture.

9 Wat Phra Kaeo Museum

This museum *(see p13)* displays a treasure trove of artifacts salvaged from restoration of the palace, such as former costumes of the Emerald Buddha.

10 Queen Sirikit Museum of Textiles

Formerly the site of the Royal Treasury, this building, constructed from white Italian marble, now houses a textile museum. On display is ceremonial and modern royal attire, with an emphasis on Thai silk garments, plus pieces from elsewhere in Asia.

Panoramic view of the Grand Palace at night

6 Phaisan Thaksin Hall

This hall is not open to the public and is used only for coronations. It contains the Coronation Chair and the tutelary deity, Phra Siam Thewathirat.

Map of the Grand Palace

8 Siwalai Gardens

These well-manicured, picturesque gardens were once used for official receptions. Located within the gardens are the Phra Buddha Ratana Sathan, built as a personal chapel by Rama IV *(see p38)*, and Boromphiman Mansion, built in the Neo-Classical style by Rama V *(see p38)* for the Crown Prince. It is now used as a guesthouse for visiting dignitaries.

ENTERING AND GETTING AROUND THE COMPLEX

Entry is via the gate on Na Phra Lan Road, where anyone inappropriately dressed is required to borrow clothes. The ticket office is outside the western wall of Wat Phra Kaeo *(see pp12–13)*, near the temple's entrance. Visitors usually walk clockwise around Wat Phra Kaeo before exiting the temple through its southern wall and exploring the rest of the Grand Palace. Allow about two hours to walk around the site.

🔟 ⭐ National Museum

Thailand's premier museum offers a great introduction to Thai history. Inside, the Buddhaisawan Chapel is one of the country's most precious treasures, as is the Phra Sihing Buddha image it houses. Other highlights include well-preserved fragments of Dvaravati and Srivijaya statues, and the royal funeral chariots.

4 Lanna Art
Several small Buddha images from northern Thailand in the Lanna period (13th to 18th centuries) are on display here.

5 Phra Sihing Buddha Image
One of three such images claiming to be the original, this small but superbly crafted Sukhothai-style sculpture sits on a pedestal in the Buddhaisawan Chapel and is bathed in a golden glow.

1 Buddhaisawan Chapel
This beautiful chapel **(above)**, built in 1787 for the Second King, now sits at the heart of the National Museum complex. Its rich murals, polished floors, gilt Buddha images, and hushed atmosphere make it a star sight.

2 Ayutthayan Art
Huge, serene Buddha heads, as well as scripture cabinets adorned with scenes of Ayutthaya in its heyday (see pp32–3), are displayed in the Ayutthayan gallery.

3 Rattanakosin Art
A gallery in the north wing displays art and furnishings from the 18th- to 20th century Rattanakosin era **(right)**. These pieces combine traditional and Western elements.

6 Red House
A fine example of an Ayutthaya-style teak house, the Red House was originally the home of Rama I's older sister, Sri Sudarak. It has a multitiered roof decorated with beautiful carvings, and the interior contains some antique royal furnishings.

7 Thailand's Past
Located in the former Sivamokhaphiman Throne Hall, this gallery contains over a hundred superbly displayed and lighted examples of the finest antiquities and treasures from Thailand.

NEED TO KNOW

MAP B3 ■ Na Phra That Road ■ 02 224 1333 ■ Chao Phraya express boat to Tha Chang ■ www.mynmv.org

Open 9am–4pm Wed–Sun

Adm B200

■ Join the free guided tours in English, French, German, and Japanese at 9:30am on Wednesdays and Thursdays.

■ The museum covers a big area, but there are seats in shaded corners between galleries where you can take a break.

■ There is a café right at the museum entrance where you can buy snacks, ice creams, and cold drinks.

8 Sukhothai Art

Sukhothai art (dating from the mid-13th century to the mid-15th century) is often described as the apex of Thai artistic skill. The flowing lines of walking and sitting Buddha images **(right)** inside the museum bear testament to this idea.

9 Royal Funeral Chariots Gallery

The elaborately decorated carriages in this gallery give an idea of the pomp and ceremony that accompany royal funerals. Each of the gilded teak carriages weighs several tons and needs hundreds of men to pull it.

ORIGIN OF THE NATIONAL MUSEUM

The National Museum was originally the Wang Na (Palace of the Front), built in 1782 by Rama I for his younger brother and deputy. However, in 1887, Rama V decided to turn the building into a public museum so that his subjects could appreciate their rich cultural heritage.

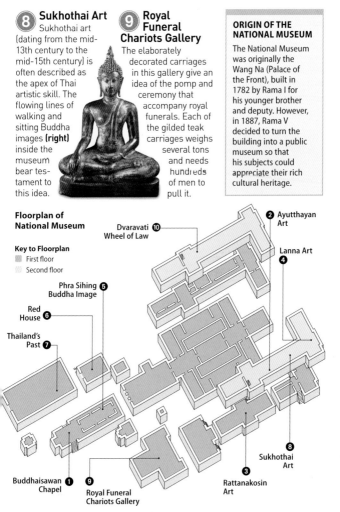

Floorplan of National Museum

Key to Floorplan
- First floor
- Second floor

- Dvaravati Wheel of Law ⑩
- ❷ Ayutthayan Art
- Lanna Art ❹
- Phra Sihing Buddha Image ❺
- Red House ❻
- Thailand's Past ❼
- ❽ Sukhothai Art
- Buddhaisawan Chapel ❶
- ❾ Royal Funeral Chariots Gallery
- ❸ Rattanakosin Art

⑩ Dvaravati Wheel of Law

Dvaravati art flourished from the 6th to the 9th centuries, and this 8th-century stone wheel **(left)** set above a deer is a great example. Located on the second floor of the south wing, it represents the Buddha's first sermon in Sarnath, India.

TOP 10 ⭐ Wat Pho

Bangkok's oldest and largest temple, Wat Pho contains the awe-inspiring Reclining Buddha. Built in the 16th century and reconstructed by Rama I, it is a typical Thai temple, with resident monks, a school, massage pavilions, and a strong community spirit. Around the grounds are a large number of statues and *chedis* (stupas) glittering with mosaics.

3 Feet of the Reclining Buddha

The soles of the feet of the Reclining Buddha are inlaid with 108 *lakshanas*, or auspicious characteristics that identify the true Buddha. Crafted in shimmering mother-of-pearl, these images are a dazzling work of art.

1 Reclining Buddha

The huge Reclining Buddha **(above)**, made of brick, plaster, and gold leaf, fills the *wihan* (assembly hall) in the northwest corner of the compound. Admire its serene expression and its feet, studded with mother-of-pearl inlay.

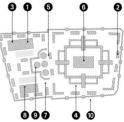

Map of Wat Pho

NEED TO KNOW

MAP B5 ▪ Soi Chetuphon ▪ 02 226 0335 ▪ Chao Phraya express boat to Tha Tien ▪ www.watpho.com

Open 8am–6:30pm daily

Adm B200

▪ Most visitors enter from Thanon Thai Wang, next to the Reclining Buddha. However, the southern entrance on Soi Chetuphon allows you to appreciate the rest of the compound in comparative peace before finally arriving at the temple's most popular highlight.

▪ Several basic food shops line the western border of the temple.

2 Traditional Massage

Wat Pho is known as a center for traditional medicine and since the 1960s has run what is considered the best massage school in Thailand. Highly trained masseurs are on hand to relieve visitors of their aches and pains. The school also offers 5-day massage courses.

4 Miniature Mountains

On several man-made mounds around the complex are statues of hermits in unusual postures. These are intended to teach people about the healing positions for the body.

5 Medicine Pavilion

In the heart of the complex, the Medicine Pavilion has stone tablets **(left)** indicating the pressure points on the body used during traditional Thai massage.

RECLINING BUDDHAS

A Reclining Buddha appears to be relaxing or even sleeping, but this interpretation could not be farther from the truth. While other images of Buddha standing, sitting, or walking show aspects of his quest to attain Enlightenment, a Reclining Buddha symbolizes his arrival at Nirvana, a state of true all-knowing awareness that is the complete antithesis of relaxation or sleep.

9 Great Chedis
There are about 100 *chedis* in the grounds of Wat Pho **(left)**, but the four most important, in the western courtyard, are the Great Chedis, which enshrine royal ashes and remains of sacred Buddha images. The *chedis* are decorated with porcelain mosaic.

6 The Bot
This ordination hall is Wat Pho's largest building. Inside, the base of the large bronze image of Buddha contains the ashes of Rama I.

7 Farang Guards
Adding a whimsical touch to this temple of learning are huge stone caricatures of Westerners, *farang* in Thai, wearing top hats **(left)**. These guards stand beside the gateways to the inner courtyard of the temple.

8 Schoolkids and Classrooms
In Wat Pho, as in many Thai temples, there is a school for children. At playtime, the compound echoes with their excited screams. Some may even try a few words of English on visitors.

10 Monks and Their Guti
Away from the most popular attractions in the complex, visitors might see monks who work at the temple **(below)**. They live in *gutis* (simple rooms) in a compound to the south of the temple.

Bangkok's Canals

In the 19th century, Bangkok was known as the "Venice of the East," since all transportation was by canal. Today, most of the canals to the east of the Chao Phraya River have been filled in to create new roads. However, the area to the west remains much as it was in the 1800s, with a network of waterways spreading out into the countryside. Here, visitors can get a taste of canalside life and visit attractions such as Wat Arun and the Royal Barge Museum.

1 Floating Vendors

Floating vendors still go from house to house in Thonburi, selling anything from hot food to plastic buckets. There is a better chance of seeing them in the morning.

NEED TO KNOW

Khlong Mon: **MAP A5**

Khlong Bangkok Noi: **MAP A2**

Khlong Bangkok Yai: **MAP B6**

Chao Phraya River: **MAP B5**

■ To tour the canals, either hire a longtail boat (about B800–1,000 per hour) from any pier, join an organized tour on a larger boat, or take the Saen Saeb Express.

■ Organized tours usually provide refreshments or make a stop where you can buy drinks and food from floating vendors.

3 Khlong Mon

Branching off from the river just north of Wat Arun, this canal leads to an orchid farm where visitors step ashore for a look around before continuing to explore the canal.

4 Boats

It is great fun to sit at a riverside café and watch the pageant of vessels flow by. Huge barges chug downstream, while small ferries nip from bank to bank, and longtail boats with bright awnings **(above)** roar past.

2 Traditional Thai Houses

Traditional houses **(below)** line the canals to the west of the Chao Phraya River. Set on stilts, they usually have an open veranda and pitched roofs.

5 Wat Arun

Established by Rama I, Wat Arun *(see pp30–31)* is known as the Temple of the Dawn. Its highlights are the five *prangs* (towers), encrusted with colorful pieces of porcelain.

Map of Bangkok's canals

Royal Barge Museum 6

This museum *(see p96)* contains a fabulous display of ornamented royal barges **(right)**, which are about 165 ft (50 m) long. Also on display are dioramas of robes worn by royal rowers and information on the use of the barges that appear in royal processions on the river.

Khlong Bangkok Noi 7

Though it is now termed a *khlong*, or canal, this waterway *(see p98)* was once the main channel of the Chao Phraya River. Near its entrance is the Royal Barge Museum and a little farther on is Wat Suwannaram, which has some rich murals.

Saen Saeb Canal 8

This canal **(right)** is quite useful for reaching the Old City from Downtown. The Saen Saeb Express boats run from Saphan Phanfa Lela to Pratunam, and beyond if you transfer.

Khlong Bangkok Yai 10

Popular with tour boats, this canal passes several temples, including Wat Kalayanamit *(see p98)*, which has a huge Buddha image, and Wat Pak Nam, famous for its amulets. Many boats also stop at a snake farm and the floating market along Khlong Dao Khanong.

Chao Phraya – River of Kings 9

Without the Chao Phraya River **(below)**, there would be no Bangkok. Named for the founder of the Chakri dynasty, Chao Phraya Chakri *(see p38)*, the river has always been the lifeblood of the nation, providing an aquatic highway for a range of boats.

RIDING THE CHAO PHRAYA EXPRESS

River buses are a great way to see the Chao Phraya and beat the traffic. The central section from Sathorn (Central) pier upstream to Phra Athit takes around 30 minutes, passing by several sights, such as the Church of Santa Cruz *(see p98)*, Wat Arun, Wat Phra Kaeo *(see pp12–13)*, and Wat Rakhang *(see p98)*. The website www.chaophraya expressboat.com has more information.

Following pages Wat Pho's elaborate Scripture Hall

TOP 10 ⭐ Damnoen Saduak Floating Market

Today, the many waterways of Bangkok's once-extensive canal network have been filled in to make new roads, but the image of floating vendors in traditional dress remains quintessentially Thai. As a result, vendors and tourists alike descend on Damnoen Saduak each morning to re-enact scenes from an idealized past. Visitors can explore the canals, take pictures, and shop for souvenirs.

5 Ton Kem Market

What is referred to as Damnoen Saduak Floating Market is actually three separate markets, the biggest being Ton Kem Market on Khlong Damnoen Saduak **(below)**. This market is very popular with both tour groups and vendors, so the canal often gets jammed with boats.

1 Fruits

Many of the *sampans* (simple, square-ended rowing boats) on the canals here sell freshly picked pomelos, bananas, rose apples, and jackfruit **(above)**.

2 Bridge

There are plenty of opportunities for taking pictures while exploring by boat, but the classic view of the floating market, busy with boats, is from the bridge at Ton Kem Market.

3 Fruit Orchards

To add variety to a visit to the floating market, many tour groups include a visit to an orchard to sample ripe fruit. Some orchards also keep harmless pythons, which tourists can drape round their necks for a souvenir photo.

OTHER FLOATING MARKETS

Damnoen Saduak gets the lion's share of visitors to floating markets, but there are other locations in and around Bangkok where similar markets operate, if only once a week. These include Amphawa, Tha Kha, Lam Phya, Don Wai, Wat Sai, and Taling Chan. The last two are near the center of Bangkok, but are exclusively for tourists.

4 Boat Noodles

It is a minor miracle that cooks can prepare a tasty bowl of *gooaydteeo rua* (boat noodles), in a small boat and serve it without spilling a drop **(below)**. These are so popular that noodle shops often display their dishes in a boat.

8 Boats

Most vendors paddle around in *sampans*, which are easily maneuvered and ideal for displaying goods for sale **(left)**. The tourists, however, are propelled around the canals in longtail boats. These boats can be noisy but will offer protection from the elements and can cover a big area in a short time.

9 Boat Vendors

The *sampans* that the vendors paddle along the canals provide no protection from the elements, so most vendors wear a *ngob* – a traditional hat that ingeniously allows for ventilation. Many also wear a type of collarless denim shirt typical in rural Thailand.

6 Hia Kui Market

A short way south of Ton Kem, Hia Kui Market has a more authentic feel to it. The banks of the canal are dotted with souvenir shops where some group tours stop for mementos.

7 Khun Pitak Market

On a smaller canal south of Hia Kui, Khun Pitak is the least crowded of the three markets, but it is still a bustling place early in the morning when the locals buy fresh produce and spices.

10 Souvenirs

With busloads of tourists arriving in Damnoen Saduak every morning, many locals operate souvenir stalls on the banks of the canals, selling traditional hats **(above)**, silk purses, carved soaps, and, of course, colorful postcards of the market.

NEED TO KNOW

MAP S2 ■ 62 miles (100 km) SW of Bangkok ■ AC minibus or bus from Bangkok's Southern Bus Terminal

■ To enjoy the market before busloads of tourists arrive (usually around 9–10am). Stay overnight in a local guesthouse and get out on the canals in the early morning.

■ Most guided tours include refreshments, but there are a large number of vendors on the canals selling food and drink for independent travelers.

TOP 10 ⭐ Chatuchak Weekend Market

Chatuchak Market, held every Saturday and Sunday, is the biggest market in Thailand. An estimated quarter of a million people visit this veritable shopaholic's paradise each day. The vast site has more than 15,000 stalls, but products are grouped by theme into a series of numbered sections, making it easy to find specific items.

1 Home Decor
Items to beautify your home **(left)** can be found in sections 2 to 7. If you wish to buy bulky items, you can ship them home via a number of shipping companies located in the market.

2 Crafts
Thailand is renowned all over the world for its handicrafts, including woodcarvings, basketware, lacquerware, ceramics, silk, silverware, and musical instruments. Such items can be found in section 8 of the market, where, with a little bit of luck, all the gifts you may need for your friends and family can be purchased in one go.

3 Plants
In sections 3 and 4 of the market you can pick up a young fruit tree or a rose bush, a sweet-smelling jasmine plant, or a delicate orchid. There are also a few stalls which sell fertilizer, flower pots, and gardening tools.

4 Chatuchak Park
If you need a break from the crowds, head to the adjacent Chatuchak Park **(below)**, just north of the market. Running the length of the park is an artificial lake. Also located nearby is the Bangkok Butterfly Garden (see p55) in Rotfai Park.

NEED TO KNOW
MAP T5 ▪ Thanon Phaholyothin ▪ Skytrain Mo Chit, MRT Subway Chatuchak Park or Kampaeng Phet ▪ www.chatuchak.org

Open 6am–6pm Sat & Sun

▪ Go to Chatuchak in the morning to avoid the worst of the heat. Bargaining is expected, and some vendors will reduce their initial prices by half.

▪ Simple maps are handed out free but serious shoppers should pick up Nancy Chandler's map of Bangkok, available at many bookstores and hotels.

▪ To eat and drink in air-conditioned comfort, head to the Dream Section, which has several modern restaurants, offering varied cuisines.

7 Central Clock Tower

The tall clock tower **(left)** in the heart of the market is a useful landmark because it is visible from many areas. If you get lost, head for this clock tower, from where it should be easier to find your way.

ENDANGERED SPECIES

Unfortunately, Thailand is a major conduit for the sale of endangered species coming from neighboring countries. Several raids on dealers in Chatuchak Weekend Market have revealed animals being kept in awful conditions, and while casual visitors are never likely to see them, this illegal trade still continues underground.

10 Antiques

Located in section 26 of the market antiques on sale, include furniture, paintings, Buddha images **(left)**, lamps, jewelry, clocks, and carvings. However, take extra care when considering a purchase. Thai craftsmen are highly skilled in creating fakes, and all genuine antiques will need the appropriate documentation for customs clearance.

5 Books

Bibliophiles will love section 1, which has remaindered art books stacked beside collectible first editions and back issues of magazines. It is best visited last as the weight of purchases may discourage further exploration of the market.

8 Artists

There is an excellent art market located in section 7. Here, visitors will find small studios producing good-value paintings as well as higher-end pieces of art. Artists can be viewed at work on original pieces, and it is also possible to commission reproductions.

9 Clothing and Accessories

The market houses around 5,000 stalls that sell either clothes or fabric **(right)**, as well as fashion accessories. Most of them are in sections 12, 14, 16, 18, and 20. With rock-bottom prices, these are some of the most popular and crowded sections of the market.

6 Food and Drink Stalls

More than 400 food and drink stalls are scattered throughout the market. Many of these stalls specialize in only one expertly cooked dish, so snacking here can be a superb gourmet experience.

TOP 10 ⭐ Jim Thompson House

Jim Thompson, an American businessman who came to Bangkok in 1945, is credited with having revived the Thai art of silk weaving. His traditional Thai house contains a fantastic selection of Southeast Asian antiques, paintings, and sculptures. Surrounded by a lush garden, the large house has actually been constructed by combining six smaller teak houses, most of which are over 200 years old.

4 Dining Room

Like the master bedroom, the dining room also enjoys lovely views of the garden. The room features several items of Ming porcelain as well as some fine paintings. The dining table, which consists of two mahjong tables put together, is laid out for a meal as it might have been during the days of Jim Thompson.

1 Drawing Room

This large and airy room looks out onto a terrace and is decorated in orange and red colors **(above)**. It houses a 14th-century sandstone head of the Buddha and wooden carvings of Burmese figures set in illuminated alcoves.

2 Jataka Paintings

Near the entrance are paintings depicting scenes from the *Jataka* tales, which show the previous incarnations of Buddha. The panels were painted in the early 1800s.

5 Spirit House

Located near the canal, the spirit house **(left)** generally has ritualistic offerings of fresh fruit, flowers and incense to pacify and appease the spirits of the land on which the house stands.

JIM THOMPSON'S DISAPPEARANCE

On Easter Day, 1967, Jim Thompson went out walking in the Cameron Highlands in Malaysia. He was never seen again. His former role in the Office of Strategic Services (OSS), a predecessor of the CIA, fueled suspicion that he was abducted by Vietnamese communists, though others suspect he was hit by a truck and that the driver buried the remains.

3 Master Bedroom

With a great view over the garden, this room is filled with sculptures, paintings of the *Jataka* tales, and photographs of Jim Thompson.

6 The Garden

Surrounding the house is a garden with cooling pools and dense tropical vegetation **(below)** including flowers, banana plants, and palm trees.

8 Ban Khrua Silk Weavers

Thompson chose this location beside Khlong Saen Saeb because a silk weavers' community **(left)** lived at Ban Khrua, on the opposite bank. This made it easy for him to oversee their work.

7 Traditional Teak Houses

The roofs of these six traditional stilted houses are steeply pitched for ventilation, and the walls lean inward to create a sense of height.

9 Dvaravati Buddha Torso

Probably the most significant example of early Asian art at the complex, this headless Buddha torso, made of limestone during the Dvaravati period (6th–9th centuries), was found in Lopburi Province. The statue is on display in the garden that surrounds the house.

10 Burmese Carvings

These intricate carvings display a high level of artistic ability. Jim Thompson's extensive collection of wooden figures includes images of *nats* **(below)**, animist spirits that were incorporated into Buddhism when it developed in Myanmar.

Floorplan of Jim Thompson House

Master Bedroom **3**
Drawing Room **1**
Dining Room **4**

Burmese Carvings **10**

Key to Floorplan
First floor
Second floor

Dvaravati Buddha Torso **9**
Jataka Paintings **2**
Spirit House **5**

NEED TO KNOW

MAP P2 ■ 6 Soi Kasem San 2, Rama I Road ■ 02 216 7368 ■ Skytrain National Stadium ■ www.jimthompson house.com

Open 9am–6pm daily Adm B200

■ Ignore any touts hanging around the house who tell you it is closed; they just want to take you shopping elsewhere so they can get a commission.

■ The branch of Jim Thompson Silk, located on the grounds, sells small souvenir items such as ties and purses, while the Jim Thompson Center for the Arts upstairs hosts fascinating temporary exhibitions.

■ The enticing wine bar and restaurant (open 10am–5pm & 6–11pm daily) offer repose next to a tranquil lotus pond.

🔟 ⭐ Wat Arun

Wat Arun is named for Aruna, the Indian god of dawn, because General Taksin arrived here at sunrise on an October day in 1767 to establish Thonburi as Siam's new capital. With its prominent *prangs* (towers), the temple shows a strong Khmer influence. All the *prangs* are ornamentally encrusted with colorful broken porcelain.

NEED TO KNOW

MAP B5 ■ 34 Arun Amarin Road, Thonburi ■ 02 891 2185 ■ Cross-river ferry from Tha Tien Pier

Open 8am–6pm daily

Adm B100

■ Viewing Wat Arun for the first time may invoke a sense of *déjà vu*. Its silhouette has been used in the official logo of the Tourism Authority of Thailand.

■ Although strolling food and drink vendors do occasionally look for business at the temple, there is no permanent café here, so it's always best to carry a bottle of water with you around the complex.

■ If you visit in the late afternoon, in time to enjoy views of the temple at sunset, you can pause for refreshment at one of the cafés on the east bank of the river.

1 Stairs on Central Prang

The steep stairs up the central *prang* represent the difficulties humans face when trying to attain enlightenment. They lead up to a terrace with a view, but the upper stairway is often closed.

2 Chinese Guards

Steps lead up to the first terrace, and each set of steps is guarded by Chinese figures that may have arrived as ballast on ships. There are also statues of many mythical creatures on the terrace.

3 River View

It may be called the Temple of Dawn, but Wat Arun's best view is seen at sunset from the east bank of the river **(below)**. There are cafés and restaurants around Tha Tien from where you can watch the sun slip down behind the temple's soaring *prang*.

4 Central Prang

The central *prang* **(above)** was extended to its current height of 266 ft (81 m) by Rama III (r. 1824–51). It represents Mount Meru, the abode of the gods in Hindu and Buddhist cosmology. It is topped with a thunderbolt, the weapon of the god Indra, who has also been depicted riding the three-headed elephant Erawan in niches on the *prang*.

5 Ceramic Details

The colorful ceramics **(above)** that cover the *prang* are an early form of recycling. In the 1800s, Chinese trading ships carried broken porcelain as ballast. When offloaded, it was used as decoration.

THE RISE AND FALL OF KING TAKSIN

Taksin the Great (r.1768–82) became one of Siam's most successful warrior kings. He waged wars with Cambodia, Laos, and the Malays, and by the 1770s he had expanded Siam to its largest-ever extent. Ousted in a coup, he was executed by being clubbed to death in a velvet sack so that royal blood would not touch the ground.

6 Kinnaris

Tucked away in small coves on the second level of the central *prang* are *kinnaris*, creatures that are half-bird, half-woman. *Kinnaris* are just one of the many Thai mythical creatures *(see p15)* depicted at the temple.

8 The Bot

The Buddha image in the *bot* or the ordination hall *(see p40)* was apparently molded by Rama II (r.1809–24) himself, and his ashes are buried in the base of this statue **(left)**. The murals were created during the reign of Rama V.

10 Symbolic Levels

The central *prang* has three symbolic levels. The base stands for *Traiphum*, all realms of existence in the Buddhist universe; the middle, *Tavatimsa*, where desires are gratified; the top, *Devaphum*, six heavens within seven realms of happiness.

7 Decoration of Minor Prangs

Representing the four great seas, these smaller *prangs* are supported by demons and monkeys. Each has a niche with a statue of Phra Pai, the god of wind, on a white horse.

9 Mondops

Between the four corner *prangs* are placed four *mondops* or shrines **(right)**. Each holds a Buddha statue from a key stage of his life – birth (north), meditation (east), preaching (south), and entering Nirvana (west).

TOP 10 ⭐ Ayutthaya

From the 14th century, Ayutthaya was the capital of an independent kingdom until the city was sacked by the Burmese in 1767. It was never restored as a capital city. Today, Ayutthaya is a UNESCO World Heritage Site, and its ruins give a sense of the city's former size and glory as well as offering an insight into Thailand's cultural heritage.

② Wat Thammikarat

One of the park's most atmospheric temples **(left)**, it has the ruins of an octagonal *chedi* (stupa), a *wihan*, and a fearsome *singha* (see p13).

③ Ayutthaya Historical Study Center

This center attempts to depict the city's history and trading relations, with models of ships, houses, and other historical objects. It also houses a model of Wat Phra Si Sanphet, a once great temple that has been reduced to ruins.

① Wihan Phra Mongkhon Bophit

This *wihan* (assembly hall) was built in the 1950s to shelter a very large bronze Buddha image that dates back to the 15th century.

④ Wat Phra Mahathat

An important temple during Ayutthaya's heyday, it continues to be one of the most evocative of all the city's sights **(left)**. It has smaller *prangs* (towers) leaning at precarious angles and a stone Buddha head encased by the roots of a banyan tree.

NEED TO KNOW

MAP T1 ■ 53 miles (85 km) N of Bangkok

Chao Sam Phraya National Museum: open 8:30am–4pm daily; adm B150

Ayutthaya Historical Study Center: open 9am–4pm Tue–Sun; adm B100

■ Most temples are open 8am–6pm daily, and entry usually costs B50 (some temples are free).

■ Some tour agencies include a boat trip either to or from Ayutthaya, the ideal way to approach the historic city.

■ The best way to get around is by bike, though many visitors opt for tuk tuks or an air-conditioned minibus.

■ Malakor restaurant, in front of Wat Ratchaburana, serves both Thai and Western dishes.

5 Chao Sam Phraya National Museum

Most of Ayutthaya's precious artifacts, including gold Buddha images, were either taken by the invading Burmese or looters. A few remaining items are on show here **(right)**.

6 Wat Phra Si Sanphet

Once Ayutthaya's most glorious temple, all that is left of Wat Phra Si Sanphet **(below)** today, are three Sri Lankan-style *chedis* alongside the ruins of the royal palace. The *chedis* contain ashes of Ayutthayan kings and are the park's highlight.

A SHORT HISTORY OF AYUTTHAYA

Ayutthaya was founded by King Ramathibodi I in 1350. Over the next four centuries, the kingdom came to dominate the region now known as Thailand, apart from in the north (where the Kingdom of Lanna maintained its independence). Traders from Europe returned home with tales of a highly organized and sophisticated society. The kingdom's end was as sudden as its beginning, and its capital was completely abandoned after being sacked by the Burmese in 1767.

Map of Ayutthaya

10 Wat Ratchaburana

Opposite Wat Phra Mahathat, this temple was built in 1424 by King Borommaracha II, and its main structure is a Khmer-style *prang*. In 1957, the crypt beneath the *prang* was opened by robbers, who made off with a horde of gold artifacts. The few items they did not take are now on display in the Chao Sam Phraya National Museum. The crypt can be reached by a steep staircase, where there are beautiful frescoes.

8 Wang Luang

Constructed in the 15th century by King Borommatrailokanat *(see p35)*, this royal palace had enough stable space for over 100 elephants. It was razed to the ground by the Burmese and only the foundations remain.

7 Wat Phra Ram

Wat Phra Ram is one of Ayutthaya's oldest temples, originally built in 1369. The main *prang*, decorated with Buddha images and mythical creatures like *nagas* and *garudas (see p13)*, was added during the 15th century.

9 Wat Lokaya Sutharam

This temple's highlight is a huge, whitewashed Reclining Buddha **(below)**, exposed to the elements. The pillars around it once supported a wooden hall which sheltered the image.

Sights In and Around Ayutthaya

 Bang Pa-In
15 miles (24 km) S of Ayutthaya ■ Open 8am–4pm daily ■ Adm

Included on many tours of Ayutthaya, this former royal summer retreat is an eclectic mix of Thai and Western architectural styles. The Aisawan Thipphaya-at pavilion that sits on a lake is its most photographed building.

Aisawan Thipphaya-at pavilion at Bang Pa-In

2 Wat Yai Chai Mongkol
1 mile (2 km) E of Ayutthaya ■ Open 8am–5pm daily ■ Adm

The main features of this temple include a huge *chedi* (stupa) erected by King Naresuan, a host of saffron-robed, laterite Buddha images that surround it, and a large Reclining Buddha set in the northeast corner of the temple grounds.

3 Wat Phanan Choeng
S of Ayutthaya ■ Open 8am–5pm daily ■ Adm

Particularly popular with Chinese worshippers because of a shrine to a Chinese princess, this temple dates back to the 14th century, and has been renovated over the years. Its centerpiece is a 62-ft- (19-m-) tall, seated bronze image of the Buddha.

4 Lopburi
44 miles (70 km) N of Ayutthaya

One of Thailand's oldest towns, Lopburi was an important center of Dvaravati culture from the 6th century onwards. Both King Narai the Great and Rama IV *(see p38)* used it as a second capital, and Narai's palace is well worth a visit.

5 Chantarakasem Palace Museum
NE corner of Ayutthaya ■ Open 8:30am–4pm Wed–Sun ■ Adm

Ayutthaya's oldest museum displays a throne platform that belonged to Rama IV, some beautiful ceramics and Buddha images, and a collection of cannons and muskets.

6 Wat Na Phra Mane
N of Ayutthaya ■ Open 8am–5pm daily ■ Adm

This temple was less badly damaged than most by the invading Burmese, who used it as a base during the siege. It is therefore one of the most interesting to explore. Inside is a large *bot* (ordination hall), which displays some fine architectural features, and a small *wihan* (assembly hall) which houses a rare Dvaravati stone Buddha.

Statue in Wat Phanan Choeng

7 Wat Phu Khao Thong
1 mile (2 km) NW of Ayutthaya

Also known as the Golden Mount, this temple's main feature is its *chedi*. It is possible to climb part of the way up the structure to get a panoramic view of the rice fields.

8 Wat Puthaisawan
S of Ayutthaya

Located across the river from central Ayutthaya, the temple has a restored 14th-century *prang* (tower), which is surrounded by cloisters that are packed with Buddha images.

9 Wat Chai Wattanaram
W of Ayutthaya

Built in the 17th century and restored in the late 20th century, Wat Chai Wattanaram is modeled on Angkor Wat in Cambodia, with a central *prang* surrounded by eight smaller ones.

10 St. Joseph's Cathedral
S of Ayutthaya

A cathedral was built here in the 17th century to accommodate the needs of foreign merchants, who were not permitted to enter the city center except by invitation. The cathedral was renovated in the 19th century and is still functional.

Interior of St. Joseph's Cathedral

KING NARAI THE GREAT (R.1656–88)

Narai is best remembered for his warming of diplomatic relations with Western countries, his sending of missions to European courts, and his selection of a foreigner, Constantine Phaulkon, as his principal advisor. It was from reports by European merchants of this era that Ayutthaya became known in the west for its richness and splendor. Phaulkon encouraged Narai to balance Dutch interests in the kingdom by inviting a French delegation to visit. However, many Siamese suspected, quite correctly as it turned out, that the French mission's main objective was to convert the king to Christianity, and on Narai's death French officials and troops were banished from Ayutthaya.

TOP 10
KINGS OF AYUTTHAYA

1 Ramathibodi
(r.1351–69)

2 Borommaracha I
(r.1370–88)

3 Borommaracha II
(r.1424–48)

4 Borommatrailokanat
(r.1448–88)

5 Ramathibodi II
(r.1491–1529)

6 Naresuan
(r.1590–1605)

7 Prasat Thong
(r.1629–56)

8 Narai
(r.1656–88)

9 Phra Phetracha
(r.1688–1703)

10 Phumintharacha
(r.1758–67)

King Narai the Great was a usurper, like most kings of Ayutthaya, and he deposed his uncle, Si Suthammaracha, to take the throne.

The Top 10
of Everything

The bustling interior of Central World
shopping mall

Moments in History	38
Buddhist Temples	40
Museums and Art Galleries	42
Spas	44
Sport and Leisure	46
Off the Beaten Path	48
Children's Attractions	50
Entertainment Venues	54
Bars and Clubs	56
Restaurants	58
Markets and Shopping	60
Bangkok for Free	62
Festivals	64

TOP 10 Moments in History

1 1767: Ayutthaya Overrun by the Burmese

After 400 years of being one of Asia's most powerful empires, the Kingdom of Ayutthaya *(see pp32–5)* was invaded by Burmese troops in 1767. Though the Burmese were expelled within a year, Ayutthaya was deemed unsafe as a capital and General Taksin chose Thonburi as the new capital of Siam (now Thailand).

2 1782: Bangkok Founded

Just 15 years later, a rebellion against Taksin's autocratic rule led to his demise. He was succeeded by General Chao Phraya Chakri who established the Chakri dynasty and acquired the official title of Rama I. On assuming the throne, his first action was to move the capital east across the river to Bangkok.

3 1851: Rama IV Crowned

After 27 years as a monk, Mongkut acceded to the throne to become Rama IV of the Chakri dynasty. Thais regard him as the man who began to modernize Siam, particularly through treaties that opened the country to trade with the West.

4 1868: Rama V Crowned

Chulalongkorn, son of Rama IV, succeeded his father as Rama V of the Chakri Dynasty when he was only 15 years old. He ruled for over 40 years and is credited with keeping Siam free from the clutches of

Rama V, King of Siam (r.1868–1910)

colonial powers such as England and France, which were carving up Southeast Asia at the time.

5 1893: First Railroad Line

Rama V carried on his father's programme of modernization, and in 1893 the country's first railroad line opened, stretching just 14 miles (22 km) to Pak Nam. The network was later extended to the south, north, and northeast of the country.

6 1932: End to Absolute Monarchy

The absolute power of the Siamese monarchy was ended by a bloodless coup in 1932, and a constitutional monarchy was established. It brought the military to power, setting the stage for the string of coups and counter-coups that has dominated Thailand's politics since.

Rama IV, crowned in 1851

7 1946: Rama IX Ascends the Throne

After the death of his brother King Ananda, who was shot in the head while in bed, King Bhumibol Adulyadej took over the throne as Rama IX. He reigned for 70 years, until his death in 2016.

8 1992: Military Government Ousted

In 1992, Thais demonstrated their displeasure publicly following a military coup. After the army gunned down many citizens on the streets of Bangkok, Rama IX intervened, resulting in the self-proclaimed Prime Minister, General Suchinda Kraprayoon, making a hasty exit and democracy being restored.

Protests against the military coup

9 2006: Thaksin Ousted

Thailand's self-styled "CEO leader" Thaksin Shinawatra swept to power in 2001 as head of the Thai Rak Thai party, inspiring people with his business acumen. However, he was ousted for corruption in a military coup in September 2006.

10 2011: Thailand's First Female Prime Minister

Thaksin's sister Yingluck was elected Thailand's first female Prime Minister, widely viewed as a proxy for her brother. She was deposed in a 2014 coup by General Prayut Chan-o-cha, who went on to oversee the succession of Rama X, King Vajiralongkorn, in 2016.

TOP 10 FAMOUS THAIS

Siamese twins Chang and Eng Bunker

1 Chang and Eng Bunker
Born near Bangkok, the original Siamese Twins (1811–74) settled in the USA, married, and fathered 22 children. They died within hours of each other.

2 Plaek Pibulsonggram
Prime Minister and military dictator for around 15 years, Pibulsonggram changed the country's name from Siam to Thailand in 1939.

3 Apsara Hongsakula
Crowned Miss Universe in 1965, this beauty queen was the first of three Thai women to win the accolade.

4 Prem Tinsulanonda
The country's Prime Minister from 1980–88, Tinsulanonda was one of the closest advisors to King Rama IX.

5 Khaosai Galaxy
The "Thai Tyson", Khaosai was WBA Super Flyweight champion from 1984 to 1992, defending his title 19 times.

6 Kukrit Pramoj
Thailand's 13th Prime Minister (1975–6) was honored in 1985 as National Artist for his literary works.

7 Anand Panyarachun
Serving twice as Prime Minister in the early 1990s, Panyarachun made overdue reforms to the Thai constitution in 1996.

8 Thongchai McIntyre
Known as "Bird," Thailand's biggest pop idol also has a film and TV acting career.

9 Thaksin Shinawatra
This former police officer and telecoms billionaire fronted the populist political movement known as the Red Shirts.

10 Chalermchai Kositpipat
The Buddhism-inspired works of one of Thailand's greatest contemporary artists include an entire temple in Chiang Rai.

TOP 10 Buddhist Temples

1 Wat Bowoniwet

Built in 1826, this temple has gained significance for being the place where Thai kings are ordained and as one of the main bases of Buddhism in Thailand. The murals inside feature some unusual themes, such as horse racing in England and Dutch windmills (see p72).

Wat Suthat's bronze Buddha

2 Wat Suthat

One of the most important temples in Thailand, Wat Suthat (see p71) was built in the early 1800s to house a 26-ft- (8-m-) tall bronze Buddha image from Sukhothai, which sits in the wihan, surrounded by murals. The galleries around the wihan hold over 150 Buddha images. The towering Sao Ching Cha, or Giant Swing, once used in a Brahmin ceremony, stands in front of the temple.

3 Wat Traimit

This gleamingly rebuilt temple (see p76) located in Chinatown is firmly fixed on the tourist trail because of the Golden Buddha, a 13th-century Sukhothai-style image made of solid gold.

4 Wat Suwannaram

On the Bangkok Noi canal in Thonburi, near the Royal Barge Museum, this Ayutthaya-style temple (see p98) was built during the reign of King Taksin. Step into the main building of the temple to see some of best temple murals in the country, including depictions of Westerners from the Ayutthaya era.

5 Wat Mahathat

Prince Mongkut was a monk in the Wat Mahathat temple (see p72) for 12 years before he became Rama IV (see p38). Today, the Wat Mahathat complex serves as the headquarters of the Mahachulalongkorn Buddhist University and also houses the reputed Vipassana Meditation Center.

6 Wat Saket and the Golden Mount

Built by Rama I in the late 1700s, this temple (see p70) has some excellent murals and a peaceful atmosphere. The main attraction, though, is the view of the Old City from the Golden Mount, a 250-ft (76-m) high man-made hill inside the temple.

7 Wat Benjamabophit

MAP E2 ■ Nakhon Pathom Road ■ 02 282 9686 ■ Open 7am–6pm daily ■ Adm

The last major temple built in Bangkok (between 1899 and 1911), this is commonly known to Western visitors as the Marble Temple because of its extraordinary Carrara marble bot. The ashes of Rama V are buried beneath the golden Buddha image inside the temple.

Wat Benjamabophit

Golden *chedi* at Wat Phra Kaeo

8 Wat Phra Kaeo

For many visitors, the highlight of their stay in Bangkok is a visit to Wat Phra Kaeo *(see pp12–13)*, to see beautiful examples of Buddhist art and architecture. This sacred temple features a glittering array of *chedis*, libraries, mausoleums, and the small jadeite Buddha that is the nation's greatest treasure.

9 Wat Ratchabophit

A blend of local and Western architecture, this temple *(see p72)* was built in the late 19th century by Rama V *(see p38)*, and its design was inspired by the circular *chedi* (stupa) at Nakhon Pathom. The temple's 141-ft (43-m) *chedi* is surrounded by cloisters, into which are set a *wihan* and a *bot* designed like an Italian Gothic chapel.

Detail of Wat Ratchabophit

10 Wat Pho

Bangkok's biggest and oldest temple, Wat Pho *(see pp18–19)* is known across the globe for its main attraction, the 150-ft- (46-m-) long Reclining Buddha. This *wat* is more typical of temples countrywide than Wat Phra Kaeo because it has resident monks who live in simple lodgings within the complex. It also runs a respected school of massage.

TOP 10 ELEMENTS OF A THAI TEMPLE COMPOUND

1 Wihan
The main assembly hall of a temple, where the head abbot gives sermons and people come to pray.

2 Bot
The ordination hall, which is usually smaller than the *wihan*. Highly decorated, it is off-limits to women.

3 Chedi
These dome-shaped religious monuments, or stupas, have relics sealed within their base.

4 Novices
Young men live as novices in the temple before being ordained as monks.

5 Ho Trai
The library in each temple stores sacred texts and is often raised off the ground to avoid flood damage.

6 Guti
These are the monks' living quarters in a temple complex – sometimes a small, austere wooden room set on stilts.

7 Murals
Temple murals depict incidents from the life of the Buddha, and some record scenes of Thai daily life.

8 Buddha Images
Usually the most highly valued Buddha image is placed in the *wihan*. Other images may sit or stand in the *bot* or cloisters.

9 Monks
These are holy men who follow the Buddha's teachings and advise lay people on their problems.

10 Bodhi Tree
This tree *(Ficus religiosa)* symbolizes Enlightenment, as the Buddha is said to have been sitting beneath a Bodhi tree when he attained Nirvana.

A Buddha's head in a Bodhi tree

TOP 10 Museums and Art Galleries

1 National Museum

An accurate overview of the evolution of Thai culture is laid out in the National Museum *(see pp16–17)* through exquisite Sukhothai, Ayutthaya, Rattanakosin, and Lanna artifacts. Don't miss the Ramkhamhaeng stone, bearing the oldest known inscription using the Thai alphabet, the Royal Funeral Chariots Gallery, and the Buddhaisawan Chapel.

2 Royal Barge Museum

Housed inside a dry-dock warehouse, this museum *(see p96)* features eight gleaming barges, each nearly 165 ft (50 m) long, that are used only for special royal events. The biggest, most important barge, *Suphannahongse*, carries the king.

3 National Gallery

Both traditional and contemporary Thai art are featured at this gallery *(see p72)*. There are also many temporary exhibitions. Temple banners are displayed in the section upstairs, and there is an art market in the courtyard each weekend.

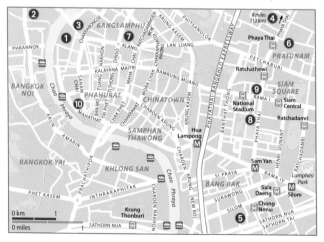

Royal Barge Museum

4 Museum of Contemporary Art

MAP T5 ▪ Vibhavadi Rangsit Road, Chatuchak ▪ 02 016 5666 ▪ Open 10am–5pm Tue–Fri, 11am–6pm Sat & Sun ▪ Adm ▪ www.moca bangkok.com

This modernist five-story museum is the pride of Thai contemporary artists, with more than 800 pieces on permanent display. Entire galleries are dedicated to the works of Thailand's most famous artists, including Chalermchai Kositpipat and Tawan Dachanee.

5 H Gallery

MAP N6 ▪ 201 Soi 12, Sathorn Road ▪ 085 021 5508 ▪ Open 10am–6pm Wed–Mon ▪ www.hgallerybkk.com

Situated in a colonial building near Silom Road, H Gallery mainly exhibits abstract works by contemporary Asian artists such as Cambodian artist Sopheap Pich's sculptures.

Traditional houses surrounded by lush greens in Suan Pakkad Palace Museum

6 Suan Pakkad Palace Museum

A compound of traditional Thai houses, Suan Pakkad Palace Museum *(see p86)* is an excellent example of Thai architecture. The houses contain antique paintings, carvings, and a stunning display of masks used in *khon* (masked theater).

7 The Queen's Gallery

MAP D3 ▪ 101 Ratchadamnoen Klang Road ▪ 02 281 5361 ▪ Open 10am–7pm Thu–Tue ▪ Adm ▪ www. queengallery.org

Established in 2003 at the request of Queen Sirikit, this gallery occupies a massive 39,825 sq ft (3,700 sq rn) of exhibition space. The Queen wanted to showcase leading examples of Thai visual art. The gallery's shop stocks an interesting range of glossy art books and T-shirts featuring contemporary art.

8 Charmchuri Art Gallery

MAP P3 ▪ Chulalongkorn University, Phaya Thai Road ▪ 02 218 3709 ▪ Open 10am–7pm Mon–Fri, noon–6pm Sat & Sun ▪ www. charmchuriartgallery.chula.ac.th

Located on the campus grounds near Siam Square at Bangkok's prestigious Chulalongkorn University is the Charmchuri Art Gallery. It features a vibrant selection of artworks created by students and professors from the university, as well as by upcoming and established Thai and international artists.

9 Bangkok Art & Culture Centre

MAP P2 ▪ Corner of Phaya Thai and Rama I Roads ▪ 02 214 6630 ▪ www. bacc.or.th

Housing several galleries of contemporary art on its upper floors, connected by spiralling ramps like New York's Guggenheim Museum, the prestigious Bangkok Art & Culture Centre *(see p62)* covers all media, from the visual arts to music and design.

10 Museum of Siam

Highly imaginative, this interactive museum *(see p72)* covers the history, art, culture and traditions of Thailand from the distant past to the present with audio-visual and traditional displays. It's a museum that kids will really love.

Interior of the Museum of Siam

TOP 10 Spas

1 Banyan Tree Spa
MAP Q5 ■ Banyan Tree Hotel, South Sathorn Road ■ 02 679 1052 ■ Open 10am–10pm daily ■ www.banyantreespa.com

Located on the 39th floor of the Banyan Tree Hotel, this deluxe spa has fantastic views and offers an extensive menu of services, including the 150-minute Royal Banyan package, comprising a herbal pouch massage, a face massage, and a herbal bath.

2 Oriental Spa
MAP M5 ■ Oriental Hotel ■ 02 659 9000/ 7440 ■ Open 9am–10pm daily ■ www.mandarinoriental.com

This spa is an oasis of calm, combining ancient Asian healing philosophies with modern Western techniques. The traditional Thai teak building is the ideal place to unwind with a massage, floral mask facial, or Oriental mud wrap.

3 Anantara Siam Spa
MAP Q3 ■ Anantara Siam Hotel, Ratchadamri Road ■ 02 126 8866 ■ Open 10am–10pm daily ■ www.siam-bangkok.anantara.com

Each suite in this spa is decorated in traditional Thai style, and some have large Roman bathtubs. The treatments include a Japanese-style bamboo massage and specific therapies for men.

Chi, The Spa, at the Shangri-La

4 Chi, The Spa
MAP M6 ■ Shangri-La Hotel ■ 02 236 7777 ■ Open 10am–10pm daily ■ www.shangri-la.com/en

Based on the design of a Tibetan temple, this spa facility is nothing less than a sanctuary of tranquility. The wide array of treatments is designed to restore *chi* (a Chinese term that refers to the universal life force that governs well-being and personal vitality). Housing some of Bangkok's largest suites, this spa offers treatments including Thai and aromatherapy massages, facials, body scrubs, detoxifying steam baths, and wraps.

5 The Oasis Spa at Sukhumvit 51
MAP T6 ■ 88 Sukhumvit Soi 51 ■ 02 262 2122 ■ Open 10am–10pm daily ■ www.oasisspa.net

This day spa is set in lush tropical gardens and is tastefully decorated with teak furniture and cotton fabrics from Bali. The wide range of treatments on offer includes facials and massages, taken individually or as

Interiors of Anantara Siam Spa

spa packages. Try the aloe and lavender body wrap or the Ayurvedic body massage.

6 The Grande Spa

MAP T6 ∎ The Sheraton Grande Sukhumvit, 250 Sukhumvit Road ∎ 02 649 8121 ∎ Open 9am–11pm daily ∎ www.sheratongrandesukhumvit.com

Located at the five-star Sheraton, this spa has an excellent reputation. Treatments combine the timeless wisdom of Thailand's healing arts with the very best of contemporary trends, and include facials, scrubs, wraps, and massages.

7 The Oasis Spa

MAP T6 ∎ 64 Sukhumvit Soi 31 ∎ 02 262 2122 ∎ Open 10am–10pm daily ∎ www.oasisspa.net

This day spa facility is set in a huge garden which helps to create an aura of calm, with birds twittering in the trees outside the treatment rooms. Options provided by the spa include an "Oasis Four Hands Massage", in which two masseurs work in unison, and the "King of Oasis", which involves massages with hot compresses and with oil.

8 Treasure Spa

MAP T6 ∎ 33 Soi 13, Soi Thonglor ∎ 02 391 7694 ∎ Open 10am–10pm daily ∎ www.treasurespa.com

This is another day spa set in a lush, tropical garden. It offers a dizzying array of treatments – massage, facial, body scrub, and body wrap, plus half-day packages. The body scrubs use tropical ingredients such as mango and lemongrass, while the aromatherapy massage employs an aromatic blend of essential oils.

9 I. Sawan Residential Spa and Club

MAP Q3 ∎ Grand Hyatt Erawan, 494 Ratchadamri Road ∎ 02 254 6308 ∎ Open 9am–11pm daily ∎ www.hyatt.com

This luxurious spa, set amid the Grand Hyatt Erawan's lovely roof gardens, offers an extensive range of treatments, each falling into one of four categories: Energy, Harmony, Purity, or Thai.

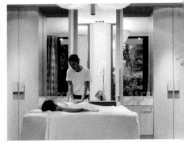

I. Sawan Residential Spa and Club

10 Health Land

MAP N6 ∎ 120 N Sathorn Road ∎ 02 637 8883 ∎ Open 9am–midnight daily ∎ www.healthlandspa.com

This chain of spas caters to those who want a good massage and other spa services in a clean private room at a reasonable price. Full spa treatments, including facials and body polishes are on offer, and the therapists are well trained.

ⓉⓄⓅ10 Sport and Leisure

T'ai chi practice at Lumphini Park

1 Martial Arts

It is possible to study and practise all kinds of martial arts in Bangkok, from Thai boxing to tae kwon do, judo, or karate, though probably the most popular is t'ai chi. To join the city's inhabitants for an impromptu session of t'ai chi or aerobics, head along to Lumphini Park (see p86) at dawn or dusk.

2 Horse Racing

The Royal Turf Club (RTC) in Dusit closed down, but the Royal Bangkok Sports Club (RBSC) continues to occupy a prime piece of downtown real estate. Races are held on alternate weekends at RBSC (see p88). The minimum bet is an impressive B50. The Silom line of the Skytrain provides a view of the RBSC.

3 Golf

This game is very popular among visitors to Bangkok for a variety of reasons – courses are generally of a high international standard, with scenic landscaping, competitive equipment rental and green fees, and attentive and friendly service. There are several courses within easy reach of Bangkok.

4 Tennis

National Stadium: MAP N2; 154 Rama I Road; 02 214 0120

A fashionable sport in Bangkok, it is best to play early in the morning or late in the afternoon to avoid the searing heat. Major hotels have private tennis courts, public courts are at the National Stadium and in Lumphini Park (see p86).

5 Takraw

Best described as volleyball played with the feet, takraw is visually exciting, with the players performing acrobatic feats to kick the ball over the net. Games are usually played early in the evening in public parks, or any small open space in Bangkok.

6 Cycling

Cycling is really popular in Bangkok. In addition to rural routes at Bang Krajao (see p97), cyclists can ride in Lumphini Park (see p86) or on the bike lanes in the Old City. Shares and rentals are available.

7 Snooker

Since James Wattana joined the world rankings, snooker has become hugely popular in Thailand. There are thousands of clubs across the country, with hundreds of them in Bangkok. Tables are usually in excellent condition, cues are on hand, and hourly rates are reasonable.

The Royal Bangkok Sports Club golf course and race track

⑧ Bowling

For a fun afternoon or evening with friends, go bowling. It offers a sporting challenge without too much exertion. Most Bangkok shopping malls have a bowling alley on the top floor, some equipped with karaoke facilities and disco lighting.

⑨ Ice Skating

Sub Zero: MAP T6; Major Cineplex Sukhumvit; 02 391 1944; open noon–9pm Mon–Fri, 11am–9pm Sat & Sun; adm

Ice rinks are rarely on a visitor's itinerary on a tropical holiday but there are a few on the outskirts. Coaches are on hand to teach beginners.

A Thai boxing match in progress

⑩ Thai Boxing

Muay Thai (Thai boxing) has enjoyed an explosion of popularity, particularly with young Westerners, many of whom spend their holidays in Thailand practising the sport in camps. Less active visitors may attend bouts at the Ratchadamnoen and Lumphini stadiums *(see p55)*.

TOP 10 THAI SPORTING EVENTS

International Kite Festival

1 Chula–Thammasat Football Match
Bangkok ▪ Jan
Held since 1934, this varsity match between two top universities features satirical parades and card stunts.

2 International Kite Festival
Hua Hin ▪ Mar
There are individual and team events at this traditional festival and a range of unusual kites are on display.

3 Chiang Mai Cricket Sixes
Chiang Mai ▪ Apr
A fun event with occasional big names.

4 Tour of Thailand
Routes vary ▪ Apr
A bicycle road race of 6 stages that draws riders from around the world.

5 Koh Samui Regatta
Chaweng Beach ▪ May/Jun
A highlight of the Asian sailing circuit.

6 Phuket Marathon
Laguna Phuket Resort ▪ Jun
Thailand's biggest marathon attracts thousands of entries each year.

7 Six Red Snooker World Championship
Bangkok ▪ Sep
Fast-paced tournament that uses six reds rather than the usual fifteen.

8 Longboat Races
Phimai & elsewhere ▪ Oct & Nov
Longboat races along town rivers.

9 Laguna Phuket Triathlon
Laguna Phuket Resort ▪ Nov
A gruelling challenge for athletes in a sport that tests their swimming, cycling, and running skills.

10 King's Cup Regatta
Phuket ▪ Dec
Since its inception in 1987, this has become Asia's premier international sailing event, and it attracts huge crowds.

TOP 10 Off the Beaten Path

1 EmQuartier Tropical Garden

MAP T6 ▪ Scala Building, 5th floor, EmQuartier Mall, Sukhumvit Road

No luxury goods are for sale in this part of EmQuartier mall – it's just an amazing rooftop garden with lavish displays of tropical plants, shaded resting spots, ponds, and a grassy meadow. The French designer, Patrick Blanc, added a rainforest chandelier as a finishing touch.

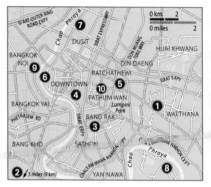

2 Wat Hua Krabeu

MAP T2 ▪ Bang Khun Tian ▪ www.wathuakrabeu.com

This amazing Buddhist temple is the work of an eccentric monk who pays tribute to the water buffalo, Thailand's traditional draft animal, by collecting their skulls – he currently has around 10,000 of them. The temple is located on a canal, and a number of passing boats offer tours.

Buffalo skulls at Wat Hua Krabeu

3 Chao Mae Tubtim Shrine

The phallic architecture found here represents fertility and good fortune. Large stone penises stand amid the trees. Women hoping for a child come here to make offerings of incense, flowers, and wooden penises to the resident spirit. This is a peaceful spot (see p88) by the Saen Saeb canal.

4 Chinatown's Soi Nana

MAP F5 ▪ Between Charoen Krung and Luang roads, Chinatown

Not to be confused with the go-go-bar area of the same name on Sukhumvit Road, this residential neighborhood buzzes with chic cafés, art galleries, bars with live music, and small restaurants. Try the Tep Bar (see p81) for innovative tunes and Thai food.

5 Sathorn Road, Sois 10–12

MAP M6

Japanese cuisine, vegetarian food and Western comfort food can be found in this cluster of chic independent restaurants and cafés on a tree-lined loop off Sathorn Road. With a range of hot nightspots (see p92) located nearby, it's very popular with young professionals, both Thai and from the expat community.

6 Queen Sirikit Museum of Textiles

Often overlooked by visitors to the Grand Palace, as it is situated on the right just after the main entrance, this superb museum (see pp12–13) displays a fine collection of textiles from throughout Asia, with an emphasis on the royal attire and the renowned and luxurious Thai silk. The grand building (formerly the Royal Treasury) gleams with white marble from Italy.

Grounds of the Floral Culture Museum

7 Floral Culture Museum

MAP S5 ▪ Yaek Ongkarak 13, Soi 28, Samsen Rd, Dusit ▪ 02 669 3633 ▪ Open 10am–6pm Tue–Sun ▪ Adm ▪ www.floralmuseum.com

Located in a lovely teak house, this museum celebrates the role of flora in Thai culture, from religious to artistic perspectives. There are cut-flower displays and paintings inside and an extensive garden outside, along with an elegant tea salon.

8 Bang Krajao

Often called Bangkok's green lung, this protected enclave *(see p97)* is on the west bank of the Chao Phraya River and is easy to reach by boat (from behind Wat Klong Toey Nok, among other piers). It's an ideal spot for cycling, with bikes available for rent, and there is also a market here on weekends. The area is also gaining a reputation for its popular eco-resort *(see p117)*.

9 Museum of Forensic Medicine

MAP A3 ▪ Siriraj Hospital, Thonburi ▪ 02 419 2601 ▪ Open 10am–5pm Wed–Mon ▪ Adm ▪ www.siriraj museum.com

Its local nickname, "Museum of Death," sums up this fascinating place. Skeletons, embalmed bodies (including the remains of a notorious serial killer), and crime-scene evidence all make for a grisly yet informative visit. Other museums exploring medicine and local history can also be found on the hospital's grounds and are worth checking out while here.

Art Deco interior of Scala Cinema

10 Scala Cinema

MAP P2 ▪ Siam Square, Soi 1 ▪ 02 251 2861

Completed in 1967, the 900-seat Art Deco Scala harks back to the pre-multiplex period and has been well restored. The best place to catch a movie in Bangkok, it shows new releases in a classic setting, and offers fantastic value for money.

Cycleway over the river in the green surroundings of Bang Krajao

🔟 Children's Attractions

Roller coaster soaring over Dream World amusement park

1 Dream World
MAP T2 ▪ 62 Moo 1, Rangsit-Nakornnayok Road, Thanyaburi, Pathumthani ▪ 02 577 8666 ▪ Open 10am–5pm Mon–Fri, 10am–7pm Sat & Sun ▪ Adm ▪ www.dreamworld.co.th

Featuring a hanging roller coaster, a sightseeing train, water rides and various other amusements, the Dream World theme park comprises different areas, including Snow Town, Fantasy Land as well as a haunted mansion.

2 SEA LIFE Bangkok Ocean World
One of the largest aquariums in Southeast Asia, the superb SEA LIFE Bangkok Ocean World (see p88) is divided into zones such as Ocean Tunnel and Rocky Shore. Attractions include glass-bottomed boat rides, underwater walks with diving helmets, as well as various tours.

SEA LIFE Bangkok Ocean World penguin

3 The Queen Saovabha Memorial Institute
Founded as the Pasteur Institute in 1923, the Queen Saovabha Memorial Institute (see p85), named after one of Rama V's wives, is now run by the Red Cross. Shows to educate the public about the dangers of Thai snakes are held every day (2:30pm Mon–Fri, 11am Sat & Sun), and venom-milking sessions of cobras and pit vipers (to produce snake-bite serums) take place on weekdays at 11am.

4 Kidzania
MAP P2 ▪ Floor 5, Siam Paragon, Rama I Road ▪ 02 683 1888 ▪ Open 10am–5pm Mon–Fri, 10:30am–8:30pm Sat, Sun & hols ▪ Adm ▪ www.bangkok.kidzania.com

Kids can play at being doctors and nurses, Japanese chefs, crime scene investigators, and even fortune tellers at this imaginative and varied activity centre in Bangkok.

5 Funarium
MAP T6 ▪ Soi 26, Sukhumvit Road, near Rama IV Road ▪ 02 665 6555 ▪ Open 9am–6pm Mon–Thu, 9am–7pm Fri–Sun ▪ Adm ▪ www.funarium.co.th

Children 13 years and under can partake in a number of activities at this huge indoor playground near the center of town. It has a four-lane slide, a trampoline, and a restaurant, and it hosts story telling, cooking classes as well as magic show events on weekends.

6 Bangkok Butterfly Garden and Insectarium

MAP T5 ▪ Suan Vachirabenchathat (Rotfai or Railway Park), Kamphaeng Phet 3 Road ▪ 02 272 4359 ▪ Open 8:30am–4:30pm Tue–Sun

Walking distance from Chatuchak Park subway station and Mo Chit Skytrain station, this park *(see p63)* is home to over 500 butterflies. There is a study centre and a children's playground on site and one can rent bikes in the adjacent park, which has family-oriented cycle routes.

Beautifully shaded Lumphini Park

8 Lumphini Park

Named after the birthplace of the Buddha in Nepal, this is the only decent-sized park *(see p86)* in the center of Bangkok. It has lots of shady trees and a large lake.

9 Children's Discovery Museum

MAP T5 ▪ Queen Sirikit Park, Kamphaengphet Road ▪ 02 246 6144 ▪ Open 10am–4pm Tue–Sun

Hands-on exhibits include a Science Discovery Zone, and Incredible Me, where children can learn about their bodies, senses, and emotions.

Exhibit at Bangkok Dolls Museum

7 Bangkok Dolls Museum

This museum *(see p98)* was created by Tongkorn Chandavimol in the 1950s after a visit to Japan, which aroused her interest in dolls from different countries and eras, which are dressed in mini-ature costumes and presented in context. The dolls here, from her own collection, are from all over the world. Handcrafted dolls can be bought in the adjacent work-shop for B500.

10 Flow House

MAP T6 ▪ A-Square, 120/1 Sukhumvit Soi 26 ▪ 02 108 5210 ▪ Open 11am–10pm daily ▪ Adm (no children under 5) ▪ www.flowhousebangkok.com

The wave-simulating surfing machine here is guaranteed to pacify the most restless of adoles-cents. There is a bit of a learning curve involved, so instructors are always on hand.

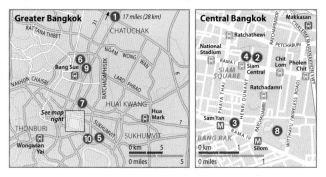

TOP 10 Entertainment Venues

A stage full of actors and dancers at the National Theatre

1 National Theatre
MAP B3 ■ **Rachini Road**
■ **02 224 1342** ■ **Adm**

Productions of Thai classical drama such as *khon* (masked theater) with skilled actors and sumptuous costumes are staged twice a month, on Sundays, at the National Theatre. An impressive medley of dances and musical shows are also performed here.

2 Siam Niramit
A cultural extravaganza designed for tourists, this show *(see p101)* presents an idealized vision of ancient Siam. Featuring over 150 performers, 500 costumes, and lots of special hi-tech effects, this show takes the audience on a spectacular journey to the enchanted kingdom of Thailand.

3 Silom Village
MAP N5
■ **Silom Road** ■ **02 635 6313** ■ **Indoor show with set dinner 8:15–9pm daily** ■ **Adm**
■ **www.silomvillage.co.th**

Accompanied by dinner (served from 7:30pm onwards), this show at the Ruen Thep hall in Silom

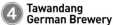

Thai dancers at a cultural show in Bangkok

Village features various forms of Thai dance. The standard of the performance and quality of the food make it a good choice for an evening's entertainment.

4 Tawandang German Brewery

Enjoy a wildly entertaining cabaret, featuring Thai as well as Western pop and folk music, ballet, hip-hop dancing, and magic shows at the Tawandang German Brewery *(see p101)*. The huge dome of this vast all-round venue can host up to 1,600 revellers and it offers good food and great micro-brewed German beer.

5 Sala Chalermkrung Royal Theatre
MAP C5 ■ **Charoen Krung Road** ■ **02 224 4499** ■ **Khon: 7:30pm Fri** ■ **Adm** ■ **www. salachalermkrung.com**

Built in 1933 by Rama VII, this was Thailand's first theater to be built with the intention of screening "talking pictures." Today this theatre is used for staging *khon* (masked theater) and for entertaining live performances by skilled singers and musicians.

6 Thailand Cultural Centre

MAP T5 ▪ Ratchadaphisek Road ▪ 02 247 0028 ▪ www.culture.go.th

Bangkok's main center for the performing arts, this state-run facility is home to the Bangkok Symphony Orchestra. It also hosts the annual International Festival of Dance and Music (see p64). International artists perform here during world tours, so check for upcoming events.

7 Ratchadamnoen Boxing Stadium

MAP E2 ▪ 1 Ratchadamnoen Nok Road ▪ 02 281 4205 ▪ Bouts: 6:30–11pm Mon, Wed, Thu; 5–8pm and 8:30pm–midnight Sun ▪ Adm

An evening of *muay Thai*, or Thai boxing (see p47) is great fun. You'll not only experience the thrill of the fight, but will also see how worked up the Thai spectators get. Add the strange pre-fight dances by the boxers to the accompaniment of wailing instruments, and you have a night of exotic Oriental fun.

8 Calypso Cabaret

Cabarets performed by transvestites are popular in Thailand. This famous show (see p101) involves an entertaining cast of ladyboys looking absolutely sensational in sequins and stockings, lip-synching and dancing to pop songs, with well choreographed dance routines.

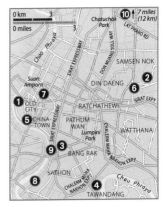

9 Sala Rim Naam

MAP M5 ▪ Mandarin Oriental Hotel ▪ 02 659 9000 ▪ Lunch: noon–2:30pm daily; dinner: 7–10:30pm daily; show: 7:45pm daily ▪ www.mandarinoriental.com

This is a custom-built facility offering a show of traditional Thai dance and a gourmet dinner. Prices are above average, but the event is memorable.

The dining area at Sala Rim Naam

10 Lumphini Boxing Stadium

In 2014, this stadium (see p101) moved out to the northern suburbs. Slightly more prestigious than Ratchadamnoen Stadium, Lumphini hosts top Thai boxing fights on Tuesdays and Fridays. Check website for upcoming fights.

A performer at Calypso Cabaret

TOP 10 Bars and Clubs

Live music at Adhere the 13th

1 Adhere the 13th (Blues Bar)

This tiny hole-in-the-wall bar *(see p74)*, popularly known as the Blues Bar, has a welcoming atmosphere, sociable pavement seats, and well-priced beer and cocktails. The Thai and expat bands play mostly blues and jazz, with special weekend events proving to be the big crowd-pullers.

2 Sky Bar

Famous for alfresco drinks, this standing-only bar *(see p92)* featured in *The Hangover II*. It is built 902-ft (275-m) above the city's pavements, with almost 360-degree views. Come early to enjoy the stunning panoramas as the sun sets.

3 Saxophone

The music here *(see p93)* is impressive with three sets every night, mixing jazz and acoustic with blues, rock, and reggae. Prices are moderate.

4 The Club@Koi

Attached to a Californian-style Japanese restaurant, Bangkok's coolest nightclub *(see p93)* pulls in a dress-to-impress crowd, with music varying by the night. There are booths, standing tables, a dance floor, and great views of the city from its 39th-floor Lounge.

5 Bamboo Bar

With its relaxed atmosphere and great lineups, this is a fantastic spot *(see p93)* to unwind and listen to smooth jazz. It has an elegant tropical atmosphere, and the attentive staff ensure they keep the drinks flowing.

6 Maggie Choo's

Discreet and opulent, the prohibition era of 1930s Shanghai has been recreated in this trendy bar *(see p93)*. Leather armchairs and couches are surrounded by Art Deco lamps and Khmer statues, and the brick walls are original – it was once a bank vault. There's live jazz later in the evenings and good food.

Shanghai prohibition-era decadence at Maggie Choo's

7 Levels

Each of the three party zones *(see p93)* at this famous nightspot has its own atmosphere and vibe, from raucous house to sophisticated lounge music. Check out all three to experience the full effect.

8 Brown Sugar: The Jazz Boutique

This long-established jazz bar *(see p74)* is one of Bangkok's iconic night-time venues. Being the city's premier jazz venue it attracts some exceptionally talented musicians. It features a nightly acoustic set followed by bands. There's an extra midnight set on Friday and Saturday, and a jam session on Sunday.

Musician playing at Brown Sugar

9 Studio Lam

This small bar *(see p100)* is run by the DJs of Zudrangma Records, who play *morlam*, folk music from northeastern Thailand, and an eclectic choice of beats from around the world on a massive, purpose-built sound system.

10 Hyde and Seek

Sophisticated, Western-style gastropub, Hyde and Seek *(see p92)* serves imported draught beers. It also offers a wide selection of wines by the glass, as well as good bar bites, pastas, and comfort food.

TOP 10 GAY BARS AND CLUBS

Gay bars in the Soi Twilight district

1 The Balcony
MAP P5 ▪ Silom Soi 4
At the heart of Bangkok's gay scene, the Balcony bar offers cheap food and great value evening happy hours.

2 The Stranger Bar
MAP P5 ▪ Silom Soi 4
This Stranger features drag shows every night, and serves great cocktails.

3 Disco Disco
MAP P5 ▪ Silom Soi 2
This bar-cum-disco is one of the top places to see and be seen in Bangkok.

4 DJ Station
A popular gay disco *(see p93)* that is packed to the rafters almost every night.

5 The Expresso
MAP P5 ▪ Silom Soi 2
This bar is a good place to chill out and take in the action in Soi 2.

6 Jupiter 2018
MAP P5 ▪ Silom Soi 4
Enjoy the live dance show at Jupiter 2018, a popular gay go-go bar.

7 G Bangkok
MAP P5 ▪ Silom Road (between Soi 2 and Soi 4)
This late-night club fills up even after the DJ Station closes.

8 Telephone Pub
MAP P5 ▪ 114/11–13 Silom Soi 4
This pub is named for the phones that once offered table-to-table contact.

9 Fork and Cork
MAP P5 ▪ 104 Silom Soi 4
The good range of food served at this bar appeals to a classy crowd.

10 Dick's Café
MAP P5 ▪ Surawong Road
Elegant day-and-night café and bar with a Casablanca theme to the decor.

Restaurants

Lavish interior at Le Normandie, with calming river views

① Le Normandie

An institution in the venerable Oriental Hotel, Le Normandie *(see p91)* serves top-notch classic French food and has a relaxing ambience, lavish decor, views on the river, and impeccable service. Specialties include duck foie gras and Brittany lobster, and the wine list offers over 200 French wines.

② Bo.Lan

Thai food at its finest is served in this beautifully renovated wooden house *(see p99)*. There are three tasting menus in the evening (including one vegetarian), and a simpler set menu at lunchtime. All offer eclectic yet authentic Thai cuisine made from the finest organic ingredients.

Thai fine-dining at Bo.Lan

③ L'Atelier de Joël Robuchon

Considered the most important chef since Escoffier, Robuchon does French food that is elegant, rustic and imaginative. L'Atelier *(see p91)* seats guests around an open kitchen. Thai cuisine influences some of the dishes. It's *très, très chic*.

④ Blue Elephant

Located in a European-style mansion, the Blue Elephant *(see p99)* offers a menu of Royal Thai cuisine, ranging from classic staples to experimental creations. There are a number of tasty starters, and the salmon larb main is highly recommended. There's also a jazzy cocktail bar.

⑤ Issaya Siamese Club

Delicious Thai food with a contemporary twist is served in a 1920s mansion *(see p91)* with private dining rooms. There's bright, quirky furnishings and a garden outside. The chef's choices are indicated on the menu, including *yam hua plii* (banana flower salad with crunchy dressing) and lamb shank *massaman* curry.

⑥ Lenzi Tuscan Kitchen

Choosing the best Italian in Bangkok is hard, but Lenzi *(see p91)* is a strong contender. The chef, formerly of the excellent Opus Wine Bar, has perfectly re-created the cuisine of his native Tuscany. The food and the service are excellent.

7 Eat Me

This art gallery and restaurant *(see p91)* has changing exhibitions on the walls and alfresco seating on the covered balconies. The truffle and Parmesan risotto and pappardelle with rabbit *ragù* are among the many international specialties here. The desserts are excellent, too.

8 Liu

A relative newcomer among Bangkok's Chinese restaurants, this place *(see p91)* is becoming famous for its Peking duck. The *dong po* (stewed pork belly and black soy sauce served with Chinese buns), is also excellent. The atmosphere is quiet and elegant.

9 Rang Mahal

Often named by Indians as the best Indian food in the city, Rang Mahal *(see p91)* has been perfecting its fare for more than 20 years. There's live but discreet Indian music in the evenings. The views from its 26th-floor perch atop the Rembrandt Hotel are incredible.

10 Gaggan

Consistently voted among the world's top 50 in *Restaurant* magazine, Gaggan *(see p91)* makes progressive Indian food using molecular gastronomy techniques. With a relaxed ambience in a converted wooden house, it has panache in both menu and service.

Relaxed dining area at Gaggan

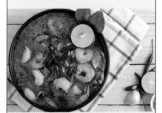

Bowl of *tom yam kung*

TOP 10 CULINARY HIGHLIGHTS

1 Tom Yam Kung
Thailand's signature dish – a hot and spicy soup with chilies, lemongrass, and galangal – is typically served with prawns or seafood.

2 Phat Thai
Literally "Thai fry," this delicious noodle dish with beansprouts, peanuts, and eggs is a great lunchtime filler.

3 Kaeng Phanaeng
This thick curry made with coconut cream and spices is usually served with pork or chicken, plus a side of rice.

4 Nam Prik Num
This delicious, gooey dip made of pounded chilies and eggplant seems to typify Thai cuisine with its spicy taste and creamy texture.

5 Sticky Rice
Thais from the north and northeast of the country often press a ball of sticky rice into their dips and sauces.

6 Som Tam
Unripe (green) papaya is shredded finely and mixed with dried shrimp, lemon juice, tomatoes, peanuts, fish sauce, and chilies to make this salad.

7 Phat Pak Bung
Morning glory, one of Thailand's tastiest green vegetables, is fried with garlic and chilis in oyster sauce for this crunchy, nutritious dish.

8 Mango with Sticky Rice
A delicious dessert of ripe mango with sticky rice and a coconut milk sauce.

9 Coconut Custard
This dessert is a sweet concoction of coconut milk, eggs, and sugar.

10 Fruit Juices and Shakes
Most Thai fruits can be served as tasty, thirst-quenching juices, or shakes when mixed with yoghurt.

Markets and Shopping

Entrance to Asiatique the Riverfront

① Asiatique the Riverfront

MAP S6 ■ Charoen Krung Road, between Soi 72 and Soi 76 ■ Open 4pm–midnight daily ■ www.asiatiquethailand.com

This open-air night market and entertainment zone has hundreds of cool boutiques, restaurants, the cabaret show Calypso (see p101), and a huge Ferris wheel. Despite being touristy, it's well done and good fun.

② Siam Paragon

This mall (see p89) connects with its two adjacent neighbours, Siam Center and Siam Discovery. While the featured items are mainly international luxury brands, there are also clothing and accessories from top Thai designers. All three offer a plethora of designer clothes, cosmetics, hairdressers, restaurants, cinemas, and book and music shops.

Siam Paragon

③ Mahboonkrong Shopping Center

While most of Bangkok's shopping malls have a clinical, international feel to them, Mahboonkrong (see p89) is totally Thai. Also known as MBK, this mall sprawls across seven floors. It is packed with stalls selling souvenirs and cheap clothes. There are also bigger outlets selling jewelry and a branch of the Japanese Tokyu Department Store.

④ Central World

Bangkok's largest mall (see p89), accessible by Skywalk from Siam Paragon, has everything from designer items to funky boutiques, bookstores, and electronic equipment in more than 500 stores. There are also some excellent restaurants, 15 cinemas, a kids' zone, and an ice-skating rink within the complex.

⑤ Pratunam

Leaving Central World, a Skywalk leads to the Pratunam area (see p88), where things move down-market a bit. Cluttering the sidewalk and spilling over into several small lanes, this bustling market is great for cheap clothes, as well as luggage, gadgets, souvenirs, and more. Platinum Fashion Mall nearby is a large air-conditioned version of Pratunam.

6 Emporium and EmQuartier

These neighboring malls (see p89) cover both sides of Sukhumvit Road, joined by a Skywalk. While the Emporium is dedicated to high fashion and some fine restaurants, the newer EmQuartier is more diverse and boutique-oriented. It also has a really lovely garden (see p48).

7 Lalai Sap Market

MAP P5 ■ Soi 5 (Soi Surasena), Silom Road ■ Open 8am–4pm Mon–Fri

For a look at a real, authentic Bangkokian's street market – away from the more luxurious tourist equivalents – head to Lalai Sap. There are small restaurants (busy with office workers at noon) and stalls selling inexpensive clothing and accessories. The market's name means "Money Melts," but it melts in small denominations here.

8 Terminal 21

MAP T6 ■ Sukhumvit Road, corner of Soi 21 (Asok Montri Road) ■ 02 108 0888 ■ Open 10am–10pm daily ■ www.terminal21.co.th

This huge mall resembles a futuristic airport terminal, and each of the nine floors is decorated in city themes, from San Francisco to Rome. Mid-range clothing and boutiques abound, as do good restaurants. The relaxed atmosphere here tends to attract a younger and more local clientele than many of the other Sukhumvit malls.

9 Pantip Plaza

MAP Q2 ■ New Phetburi Road ■ 02 250 1555 ■ Open 10am–10pm daily ■ www.pantipplaza.com

This IT mecca sells the latest computer programs as well as digital cameras and other electronics. Although it is crammed with hardware and software, the mall is rife with counterfeit products. Despite regular police raids, vendors dealing in pirated goods stay in business thanks to their customers' huge appetite for such stuff.

Clothes at Sampeng Lane Market

10 Sampeng Lane Market

The market held on this narrow street is lined with shops selling household goods, fashion accessories, shoes, and clothing. Phahurat Road (see p77) leads into Sampeng Lane (see p78), and walking from one to the other feels like hopping from India to China.

⓾ Bangkok for Free

1 Visit Temples

Most temples in Bangkok, such as Wat Mahathat and Wat Ratchabophit *(see p72)*, are free to enter and offer a pleasant respite from the clamor of the city. All that is required is respectful dress and a quiet demeanor. Remove your shoes at the entrance of the largest building, sit for a while, and absorb the calming atmosphere.

Wat Ratchabophit's entrance

2 Thai Boxing at MBK Shopping Center

MAP P3 ▪ Corner of Phaya Thai and Rama I Roads ▪ 02 620 9000 ▪ Bouts 6pm Wednesday

Authentic *muay Thai* matches *(see p47)* are held outside Tokyu Department Store and run into the evening. These are not the watered-down exhibition matches held at tourist venues – the crowd is raucous and the punches and kicks are real.

3 Puppet Show at Artist's House in Khlong Bang Luang

MAP S6 ▪ Soi Wat Thong Sala Ngarm, Thonburi ▪ 02 868 5279 ▪ Performances 2pm Wed & Fri–Sun

On the Thonburi side of the river, this place is a bit hard to find but worth the effort. A project by a local artist here keeps Thai culture alive with traditional Thai puppet shows. There are also free art exhibits and a coffee shop.

4 Phra Athit Park Aerobics

MAP C2 ▪ Phra Athit Road

Next to the Prom Phra Sumen Fort, on the Chao Phraya River, this small but beautiful park hosts informal aerobics classes starting an hour before sunset every day. A leader on stage shows the movements and gives encouragement to all the exercisers taking part.

5 Bangkok Art & Culture Centre

An oasis of calm amid the malls in Bangkok's prime shopping zone, the BACC *(see p43)* is a striking, white contemporary art museum that always has a wide choice of exhibitions and events on. There's usually an interesting exhibition on here, as well as a performance in one of the performance spaces.

6 Thai Dancing at Erawan Shrine

This holy shrine *(see p86)* in Bangkok's shopping district venerates the Hindu God Brahma. Thais come to make offerings of flowers and incense. They also commission the resident Thai classical dancers to perform for the spirits.

Thai dancers at Erawan Shrine

T'ai chi practitioners in Lumphini Park

⑦ Lumphini Park T'ai Chi

As soon as dawn breaks, aficionados of this ancient Chinese dance-like practice start their routines (see p86). Visitors are always very welcome to participate: simply stand at the back of the group and follow the movements.

⑧ Bangkok Butterfly Garden

A respite from the nearby weekend market, this park (see p51) within a park has open areas where the butterflies live, as well as displays of various specimens under glass.

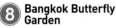

Bangkok Butterfly Garden

⑨ Neilson Hays Library Art Galleries

MAP N5 ▪ 195 Surawong Road ▪ 02 233 1731 ▪ Open 9:30am–5pm Tues–Sun ▪ www.neilsonhayslibrary.com

Housed in a beautiful Neo-Classical building, the private Neilson Hays Library has two excellent art galleries: the Rotunda and the Garden Café.

⑩ Meditation Course at Wat Mahathat

Introductory walk-in courses in Buddhist meditation start at 7am, 1pm, and 6pm and cover both seated and walking techniques. A brief lecture introduces the three-hour session. The temple (see p72) also offers longer residential courses, with food and accommodation provided; a donation is usually expected for these courses.

TOP 10 BUDGET TIPS

1 Get a local SIM card for your phone or tablet. Kiosks offer short-term plans at the airport and in all city malls. Data speeds are very good in Bangkok.

2 If you make any significant purchases, you can get a refund of the 7 percent VAT when leaving Thailand.

3 Bangkok's mass transit systems – the MRT, BTS Skytrain, and Airport Rail Link – cover most of the city.

4 The Chao Phraya Express Boat Service is a great way to see all the river sights and beat the traffic.

5 *Bangkok 101* and *The Big Chilli* are great magazines (and websites) that feature free events and promotions in the city. *BK* magazine and its website is more listings-driven, but is free.

6 Guesthouses such as the A-One Inn (see p116) are clean and cheap.

7 Bargaining is perfectly appropriate for any non-food item in a street market. Offer 50 percent and keep on smiling.

8 Imported alcoholic drinks are taxed up to 400 percent here, but the local beers (such as Singha, Leo, and Chang) are good, as is the rum – try Sang Som with soda and a squeeze of lime.

9 Traditional massage venues do not offer the luxury that you will find in the spas, but these ubiquitous shops offer good body or foot massages at very reasonable prices.

10 All shopping malls have air-conditioned food courts, often in the basement, where a variety of vendors offer local specialties for much less than you would pay in restaurants.

Food court of Siam Paragon

ᴛᴏᴘ**10** Festivals

Revellers watching the colorful lion dance during Chinese New Year

1 Chinese New Year
Chinatown ▪ Jan or Feb

This week-long Thai-Chinese celebration has lion dances in the street, lots of loud firecrackers, and colorful activities in temples.

2 Makha Puja
Citywide ▪ Feb or Mar

This annual Buddhist festival, held at the full moon, celebrates the Buddha's first sermon to 1,250 disciples, starting the dissemination of the *dhamma*.

Monks observing Makha Puja

3 Songkran
Citywide ▪ Mid–Apr

Thai New Year is the country's most chaotic and raucous festival. People throw water over each other as a symbolic form of cleansing to usher in the new year, and passers-by are not spared. Perhaps for its novelty value, this festival is particularly popular among foreign visitors.

4 Royal Ploughing Ceremony
Sanam Luang ▪ Early May

This annual event is designed to give an auspicious start to the new planting season. Sacred white oxen are used to plough a ritual field in Sanam Luang *(see p69)* near the Grand Palace *(see pp12–13)*, which is then sown with rice seeds blessed by the king. Farmers rush to collect the seeds to plant in their own fields.

5 Visakha Puja
Citywide ▪ May

The holiest day of the Buddhist calendar commemorates the Buddha's birth, enlightenment, and death. Occurring on the day of the full-moon, the evening candlelit procession around the temple is notable, especially at Wat Benjamabophit *(see p40)*.

6 International Festival of Dance and Music
Thailand Cultural Centre ▪ Sep & Oct

Since 1999, Bangkok's premier international arts festival has been held at the Thailand Cultural Centre *(see p55)* in September and October each year. It features acts from around the world, along with some of Thailand's best performers. The focus of the festival is mainly on opera, ballet, and classical music, though jazz and modern dance are represented as well.

7 Loy Krathong
Citywide ▪ Nov

This festival, usually held in November, offers homage to the goddess of the waters for providing a successful harvest. Beautiful *krathong* (small decorated floats) are released onto the river at night while fireworks light up the sky.

8 Wat Saket Fair
Golden Mount ▪ Nov

Temple fairs in Thailand are like village fêtes in the West, and this one at Wat Saket and the Golden Mount *(see p70)*, held just before or after Loy Krathong, is a good example. It has a great atmosphere, with music, theater and lots of kids having fun.

Performers at Wat Saket fair

9 Cat Expo
Wonderworld Fun Park ▪ Nov

Formerly known as Fat Festival, this is Thailand's biggest Indie music event that features more than a hundred established as well as emerging bands. There are booths where you can meet the bands, and watch films.

10 King Bhumibol's Birthday
Citywide ▪ Dec

Celebrated on December 5, this is both a national holiday and Fathers' Day, Thais have long celebrated the birthday of Rama IX, who died in late 2016. It's possible that this will remain on the calendar, with the new king Vajiralongkorn's birthday on July 28 added as a further holiday.

TOP 10 UP-COUNTRY FESTIVALS

Chiang Mai Flower Festival parade

1 Chiang Mai Flower Festival
First weekend, Feb
A parade of marching bands precedes floats bedecked with flowers.

2 ASEAN Barred Ground Dove Festival
First week, Mar
This dove-singing contest attracts competitors from far and wide to Yala.

3 Pattaya Music Festival
Mar
Thai musicians and international acts play in a wide variety of styles.

4 Poy Sang Long
First weekend, Apr
A Shan festival held in Chiang Mai and Mae Hong Son in which ordaining novices are paraded round the streets.

5 Rocket Festival
May
In the northeast, especially Yasothon, home-made rockets are fired to trigger the start of the monsoons.

6 Hua Hin Jazz Festival
May
This beach festival attracts big names.

7 Phi Ta Khon
Jun/Jul
Locals in Dan Sai dress as spirits for this wild and colorful event in Loei province.

8 Phuket Vegetarian Festival
Oct
Bizarre acts of self-mortification draw in the crowds for nine days.

9 Lanna Boat Races
Oct/Nov
At the end of the Buddhist Lent; the most exciting are in Nan Province.

10 Elephant Round-Up
Nov
Surin, in the northeast, is the venue for this pachyderm extravaganza.

Bangkok
Area by Area

The modern, glittering skyline
of Bangkok after dark

Old City	**68**
Chinatown	**76**
Downtown	**84**
Greater Bangkok	**94**
Beyond Bangkok	**102**

TOP 10 Old City

Bangkok's historical and spiritual heart lies in the Old City. When Chao Phraya Chakri, later pronounced Rama I, assumed the throne in 1782, he had a canal dug across a neck of land on the east bank of the Chao Phraya River to create an island that emulated the former capital at Ayutthaya. This island became known as Rattanakosin; now, it and the area to its east are known as the Old City. Here stand the Grand Palace, once home of the royal family, and Wat Phra Kaeo, a glittering temple that houses the Emerald Buddha, as well as several important temples, museums, universities, and Sanam Luang.

Wheel from royal funeral chariot

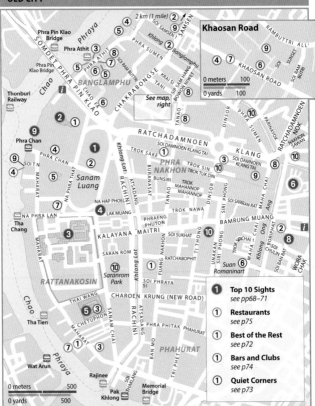

OLD CITY

Khaosan Road

1	Top 10 Sights see pp68–71
1	Restaurants see p75
1	Best of the Rest see p72
1	Bars and Clubs see p74
1	Quiet Corners see p73

1 Sanam Luang
MAP B3 ▪ Na Phra Lan Road

Considering Bangkok's congested streets and high-rise buildings, it is amazing that a large open area such as Sanam Luang, or Royal Field, could exist at all. Its importance for certain royal ceremonies, such as cremation rites of royalty, guarantee that this precious patch of land will never be developed into offices or malls. From February to April, people fly kites here, and fortune tellers ply their trade.

2 National Museum
Located near the northern end of Rattanakosin Island, the National Museum (see pp16–17) is the repository of significant Thai art. Its huge size reflects the depth of Thai artistic achievement. Exhibits range from Dvaravati sculptures over 1,000 years old, to lavish funeral chariots, and the delightful Buddhaisawan Chapel, which houses the Phra Sihing Buddha image, considered second in importance only to the Emerald Buddha in Wat Phra Kaeo.

3 Grand Palace and Wat Phra Kaeo
In the center of Rattanakosin Island, the huge complex that contains the Grand Palace and Wat Phra Kaeo (see pp12–15) is one of Asia's unforgettable sights. It is the best place for an introduction to Thai architecture and art. While the palace is strongly influenced by Italian Renaissance architecture, the temple complex is totally Thai, from the towering *bot* (ordination hall) that holds the Emerald Buddha to the slender lines of the Phra Si Rattana Chedi and the *Ramakien* murals that decorate the galleries on all sides.

Majestic facade of Wat Phra Kaeo

4 Lak Muang
MAP C4 ▪ Corner of Ratchadamnoen and Lak Muang roads ▪ Open 8:30am–5:30pm daily

This shrine houses the city pillar of Bangkok, erected by Rama I in 1782 and believed to contain the city's guardian spirit, Jao Pho Lak Muang. Also in the shrine is the city pillar of Thonburi, now part of Greater Bangkok. Both pillars are made of wood with lotus-shaped crowns and are painted gold. Lak Muang is always busy with devotees.

City pillars at Lak Muang

5 Wat Pho
Officially Wat Phra Chetuphon, this (see pp18–19) is Bangkok's oldest and largest temple and a welcoming center of learning, particularly of the massage techniques for which it is famous. While Wat Phra Kaeo impresses with bejeweled monuments, Wat Pho's charms are more subtle. The main attraction is the 150-ft (46-m) long Reclining Buddha that fills a *wihan* (assembly hall) in the compound's northwest corner, but it can be just as much fun exploring quieter corners of the grounds and chatting with the monks, schoolchildren, and massage practitioners.

⑥ Wat Saket and the Golden Mount

Wat Saket: MAP E3 ▪ Golden Mount: MAP D3; 344 Chakkaphatdi Phong Road; 02 621 2280; open 7:30am–7pm daily; adm (for Golden Mount)

This was one of the first temples built when the city was founded in the late 1700s, initially as a crematorium for the common people. Fine murals adorn the walls of the *wihan* (assembly hall). Climb the 320 steps to the summit of the Golden Mount, a 250-ft (76-m) high artificial hill surmounted by a graceful golden, bell-shaped *chedi* (stupa), for fine views of the Old City skyline.

Bowls being made at Soi Ban Baat

SPIRITS IN THAI SOCIETY

Lak Muang, the Amulet Market, and spirit houses (shrines dedicated to the spirit of the land on which a house is built) are all animist manifestations, which demonstrate that Thai religious belief is not limited to Buddhism. In fact, Buddhism's success here is partly due to its assimilation of aspects of other belief systems, such as Hinduism.

⑦ River and Canal Tour

Many visitors to Bangkok want to take a trip on the river and nearby canals *(see pp20–21)* to get a sense of how the city was before the motor car and catch a glimpse of traditional canal-side life. There are many tours that may be organized via your hotel or guesthouse. Alternatively, negotiate a price with a longtail-boat owner at any of the principal piers, and arrange a customized tour.

⑧ Soi Ban Baat

MAP D4 ▪ Soi Ban Baat, Boriphat Road

Buddhist monks have few material possessions – the *baat* (alms bowl) is one of them. Early each morning the bowls are filled with food offerings by devout Buddhists. They are mostly made in factories, but in Soi Ban Baat, or Monk's Bowl Village, there are still a few families that beat out the bowls by hand. Traditionally, these *baat* are made of eight strips of metal to represent the Eightfold Path of Buddhism. First, they are welded in a kiln, then shaped and filed smooth, and finally fired again.

⑨ Amulet Market

MAP B4 ▪ Maharat Road and small lanes ▪ Open 8am–6pm daily

There is a strong belief among Thais that small images of the

Boating down a canal

Buddha, famous kings, or even tigers' teeth worn as pendants can provide protection from misfortune. It is, therefore, quite common to see people wearing a string of such amulets around the neck, and some even become ardent collectors of amulets. One of the best places to see this faith demonstrated is in the Amulet Market on the streets around Wat Mahathat, where potential buyers will carefully scrutinize the tiny objects with magnifying glasses and quiz the vendor to ascertain the amulet's properties.

Traditional art at Wat Suthat

⑩ Wat Suthat
MAP D4 ▪ 146 Bamrung Muang Road ▪ 02 224 9845 ▪ Open 9am–4pm daily ▪ Adm

Begun in 1807 by Rama I (r.1782–1807) and completed by his successors, Wat Suthat is one of Bangkok's most important temples. Fronted by the towering Sao Ching Cha, a giant swing that was once used for a Brahmin ceremony, the compound has the tallest *wihan* in the city, especially constructed to accommodate the Phra Sri Sakyamuni Buddha, a 26-ft (8-m) tall 14th-century Sukhothai image. The murals in the *wihan* are beautifully detailed, and the temple grounds include four lovely bronze horses.

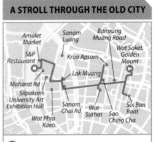

A STROLL THROUGH THE OLD CITY

▶ MORNING

Begin your exploration of the Old City at **Wat Saket**, where you can climb the **Golden Mount** to enjoy a wonderful, panoramic view of the area. From here walk south along Boriphat Road until you reach **Soi Ban Baat**, where alms bowls are beaten out of strips of metal. Go back up Boriphat Road, then left into **Bamrung Muang Road** *(see p72)* where shops sell Buddha images and temple paraphernalia. When you reach the unmissable giant swing known as Sao Ching Cha, turn into **Wat Suthat** and appreciate the superb carvings and paintings on display. Go over the canal and turn right onto Sanam Chai Road for the lush green lawns of **Sanam Luang** *(see p69)*. For lunch, head north up Dinsor Road and join the civil servants at **Krua Apsorn** *(see p75)*, tuck into fiery and authentic central Thai dishes such as green curry with fish balls.

AFTERNOON

Return to Bamrung Muang Road and head west. Straight ahead stands the **Lak Muang** *(see p69)* shrine where you can watch supplicants making offerings and praying to Bangkok's city pillar. Wander west again between Sanam Luang and **Wat Phra Kaeo** *(see pp12–13)*, to admire paintings at the **Silpakorn University Art Exhibition Hall** *(see p73)*. Buy a lucky charm at the fascinating **Amulet Market** or in the small lanes off it. Have a cool drink at **S&P Restaurant** *(see p75)* by the riverside Tha Maharaj mall at Maharat Pier to round off your day's wander in the Old City.

See map on p68 ←

The Best of the Rest

1 Wat Ratchabophit
MAP C4 ▪ Fuang Nakhon Road ▪ 02 221 1888 ▪ Open 5am–8pm daily; ordination hall: open 9–9:30am & 5:30–6pm daily

The highlights here (see p41) include inlay work on the doors and windows of the *bot* (ordination hall), and colorful tiles in the cloisters.

Inlay work at Wat Ratchabophit

2 Bamrung Muang Road
MAP D4

Originally an elephant trail, this was one of the first roads to be paved in Bangkok. Its shops sell temple necessities such as monks' robes, candles, incense, and Buddha images.

3 Museum of Siam
MAP C5 ▪ Sanam Chai Road ▪ 02 225 2777 ▪ Open 10am–6pm Tue–Sun ▪ Adm ▪ www.museum siam.org

Spread over three floors, this museum has fascinating interactive exhibits that explore Thai history and culture, Buddhism, and more.

4 Phra Sumen Fort
MAP C2 ▪ Phra Athit Road

This octagonal brick-and-stucco fort, one of 14 watchtowers, was built in 1783 to defend the city from attack.

5 Wat Mahathat
MAP B3 ▪ Maharat Road ▪ 02 221 5999 ▪ Open 7am–8pm daily

This royal temple (see p40) is home to the respected Vipassana Meditation Center.

6 National Gallery
MAP C3 ▪ 4 Chao Fa Road ▪ 02 281 2224 ▪ Open 9am–4pm Wed–Sun ▪ Adm

Located in a building that once housed the Royal Mint, this is Bangkok's principal art gallery. It features the work of established and emerging Thai artists.

7 Khao San Road
MAP C3

Besides several budget guesthouses, this bustling backpacker's ghetto has a variety of souvenir shops, market stalls, and restaurants.

8 Wat Bowoniwet
MAP C2 ▪ 240 Phra Sumen Road ▪ 02 280 0869 ▪ Open 8am–5pm daily ▪ www.watbowon.org

The base of the Thammayut sect of Buddhism, this temple (see p40) has some striking murals.

9 Loha Prasat and Wat Ratchanadda
MAP D3 ▪ 2 Maha Chai Road ▪ 02 224 8807 ▪ Open 9am–5pm daily

The Loha Prasat (or "iron castle") is a stepped, seven-tiered pyramid with 37 metal spires. Its grounds are shared with Wat Ratchanadda.

10 King Prajadhipok (Rama VII) Museum
MAP D3 ▪ 2 Lan Luang Road ▪ 02 280 3413 ▪ Open 9am–4pm Tue–Sun

This museum looks at the reign of Rama VII (1925–35), which saw the transition of Siam from absolute to constitutional monarchy.

Phra Sumen Fort

Quiet Corners

1 Buddhaisawan Chapel, National Museum

After learning about Thai history in the National Museum (see p16), settle down on the cool teak floorboards of this chapel to meditate, in front of the Phra Sihing Buddha image.

Artwork, Buddhaisawan Chapel

2 Sanam Luang

 This open grassy area (see p69) has several benches in the shade of trees that offer rest to weary legs.

3 Massage Pavilion, Wat Pho

Traditional Thai massage is a great help for aching legs and a muddled mind. Come here (see p18) for some of the country's best masseurs.

4 Thammasat University

MAP B3 ▪ Maharat Road

Thailand's second-oldest university, opened in 1934, lies just upstream from the Amulet Market. There are some nice spots for resting, and a food court catering to the students.

5 Santichaiprakhan Park

MAP C2 ▪ Phra Athit Road
▪ Open 5am–10pm daily

Looking out over the Chao Phraya River, this park makes an excellent place to sit and see the world go by. Visitors can also join the aerobics class held here at dusk every day.

6 Romaninart Park

MAP D4 ▪ Maha Chai Road
▪ Open 5am–9pm daily

Formerly the site of a prison, this park now has ponds, fountains, and shaded paths.

7 Silpakorn University Art Exhibition Hall

MAP B4 ▪ Na Phra Lan Road
▪ 02 221 3841 ▪ Open 9am–pm Mon–Fri, 9am–4pm Sat

Set inside the country's leading art school, this tranquil gallery features works by teachers, students, and artists-in-residence at the university.

8 Mahakan Fort

MAP D3 ▪ Maha Chai and Ratchadamnoen roads

This octagonal fort is one of two surviving watchtowers of the 14 that ringed the city in the late 18th century. The park beside it is a great place to stop and relax.

9 Riverside Restaurants, Tha Maharaj

MAP B3 ▪ Maharat Road

The cool river breeze makes this complex of restaurants in Tha Maharaj shopping mall, is one of the best places to recover from a tiring walk.

Walking in tranquil Saranrom Park

10 Saranrom Park

MAP C4 ▪ Rachini Road
▪ Open 5am–9pm daily

With shady trees, fountains, and benches, this park is a great place to take a break after trekking round the Grand Palace or Wat Pho (see pp12–15).

See map on p68

Bars and Clubs

1 Phra Nakorn
MAP C3 ▪ 58/2 Soi Damnoen Klang Tai ▪ 02 622 0282 ▪ Open 6pm–1am daily

Popular with artists, this bar offers views of the Golden Mount from the roof terrace. The first floor features regular exhibitions.

Outdoor seating at Adhere the 13th

2 Adhere the 13th (Blues Bar)
MAP C2 ▪ 13 Samsen Road ▪ 08 9769 4613 ▪ Open 6pm–midnight daily

Small neighborhood bar (see p56) with live blues and jazz bands nightly.

3 Sheepshank
MAP B2 ▪ Phra Athit express-boat pier ▪ 02 629 5165 ▪ Open 5pm–1am Mon, 11–1am Tue–Sun

Cool industrial-looking gastropub set in an old boat repair yard by the river. It serves American and Japanese craft beers.

4 Hippie de Bar
MAP C3 ▪ 46 Khao San Road ▪ 08 1820 3762 ▪ Open 4pm–2am daily

A fashionable courtyard bar and boutique with a retro look, Hippie de Bar attracts a diverse crowd.

5 Jazz Happens
MAP B2 ▪ Phra Athit Road ▪ 08 4450 0505 ▪ Open 5pm–1am Fri–Wed

There's live jazz every night at this cozy grassroots bar with sociable pavement tables.

6 The Club
MAP C3 ▪ 123 Khao San Road ▪ 02 629 1010 ▪ Open 10pm–3am daily

A lively atmosphere, vast dance floor, and music from techno to trance pull in the crowds here.

7 Bottle Rocket
MAP C2 ▪ 76/1 Phra Arthit Road ▪ 08 6085 5550 ▪ Open 5pm–midnight Tue–Sun

A small bar, Bottle Rocket offers Thai, Japanese as well as international craft beers on tap, and in bottles.

8 Madame Musur
MAP C2 ▪ Soi Ram Bhuttri ▪ 02 281 4238 ▪ Open 9am–midnight daily

The ambience is relaxed at Madame Musur. It serves authentic northern Thai food and a variety of drinks.

9 Roof Bar
MAP C3 ▪ 3rd floor, Centre Point Plaza, Khao San Road ▪ 08 6777 1117 ▪ Open 4:30pm–1:30am daily

Watch live bands with an amazing view from the balcony. It's a great spot to enjoy fresh air and good fun.

10 Brown Sugar: The Jazz Boutique
MAP D3 ▪ 469 Wanchad Junction, Phra Sumen Road ▪ 02 282 0396 ▪ Open 5pm–1am Tue–Thu & Sun, 5pm–2am Fri–Sat ▪ www.brown sugarbangkok.com

Enjoy live music at one of Bangkok's famous jazz bars (see p56).

Brown Sugar: The Jazz Boutique

Restaurants

PRICE CATEGORIES

For a meal for one with one or two dishes
and a soft drink, including service.

B under B200   **BB** B200–1,000
BBB over B1,000

1 Err
MAP B5 ▪ Soi Maharat, Maharat
Road ▪ 02 622 2292 ▪ Open Tue–Sun
11am–4pm & 5–9pm ▪ BB

A streetfood branch of Bo.Lan (see
p58), Err serves up delicious "urban
rustic" dishes in a retro ambience.

2 Kaloang Home Kitchen
MAP D1 ▪ 2 Soi Wat
Tevarakunchorn ▪ 02 281 9228
▪ Open 11am–10pm daily ▪ BB

Hidden behind the National Library,
this simple, alfresco riverside venue
offers guests an excellent menu
of inexpensive Thai cuisine.

3 Methavalai Sorn Daeng
MAP D3 ▪ 78/2 Ratchadamnoen
Khlang Road ▪ 02 224 3088 ▪ Open
10:30am–10pm daily ▪ BB

Open since 1957, and now a
rewarded Michelin star restaurant,
this place is popular with the
older generation of Thais. Expect
starched white tablecloths and
high-class Thai cuisine.

4 S&P, Maharat Pier
MAP B3 ▪ Maharat Pier
▪ Open 10am–10pm daily ▪ B

Part of a countrywide chain of
restaurants, S&P turns out tasty
Thai food, ice creams, and cakes.
A breezy riverside terrace is part
of the appeal at this branch.

5 Aquatini
MAP B2 ▪ Navalai River Resort,
45 Phra Athit Road ▪ 02 280 9955
▪ Open 6:30am–midnight daily
▪ www.navalai.com ▪ BB

On a breezy riverfront deck, this
hotel restaurant (see p115) serves
reasonably priced Thai food,
especially seafood.

6 Hemlock
MAP B2 ▪ 56 Phra Athit Road
▪ 02 282 7507 ▪ Open 3pm–midnight
Mon–Sat ▪ BB

A small, trendy café, Hemlock offers
many unusual dishes, including
several vegetarian options.

7 Supanniga Eating Room
MAP B5 ▪ Riva Arun Hotel, 392/
25–26 Maharat Road ▪ 02 714 7608
▪ Open 11:30am–10pm daily ▪ BB

With a terrace facing Wat Arun, this
riverside restaurant-bar serves
dishes from northern Thailand as well
as flavorful cuisine of Chanthaburi.

Diners relaxing at May Kaidee

8 May Kaidee
MAP C3 ▪ 59 Tanao Road
▪ 02 629 4413 ▪ Open 9am–10pm
daily ▪ www.maykaidee.com ▪ B

This restaurant serves delicious
and cheap vegetarian, vegan, and
raw dishes. It also has its own
cookery school.

9 Somsong Pochana
MAP C2 ▪ 173 Samsen
Road ▪ Open 9am–4pm daily ▪ B

Traditional Sukhothai-style noodles
are served to diners at this excellent
little lunch spot.

10 Krua Apsorn
MAP D3 ▪ Dinsor Road ▪ 02 685
4531 ▪ Open Mon–Sat 10:30am–8pm
▪ B

A simple restaurant, Krua Apsorn is
perfect to sample authentic and varied
Thai cuisine, especially seafood.

See map on p68

TOP10 Chinatown

At the time of Bangkok's founding in 1782, Chinese immigrants were moved out of Rattanakosin Island to make way for the Grand Palace and government buildings. They settled to the south of Rattanakosin Island beside the Chao Phraya River. These days Chinatown is one of the most colorful and congested areas of the city, and though it lacks the grand monuments of the Old City, it is fascinating for its maze of alleys, markets, gaudy temples, and gold shops. Sharing this crowded part of the capital with the Chinese is a small community of Indians in a sub-district known as Little India, with the cloth market of Phahurat at its heart.

Golden Buddha, Wat Traimit

1 Golden Buddha, Wat Traimit

MAP F6 ▪ 661 Charoen Krung Road ▪ 02 225 9775 ▪ Open 8am–5pm daily ▪ Adm

There are thousands of gold-leaf smothered Buddha images in Thailand, but the Golden Buddha is made of solid gold – all 12,000 lb (5,500 kg) of it. This fact was revealed only in 1955 when it was accidentally dropped, exposing its gold interior. The 13-ft (4-m) tall, 13th-century Sukhothai Buddha is housed in a glittering, three-story shrine.

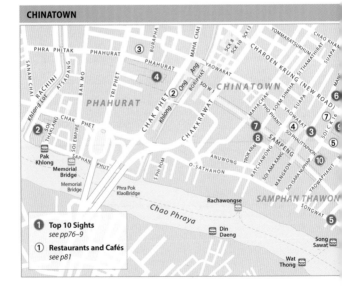

CHINATOWN

1 **Top 10 Sights**
see pp76–9

1 **Restaurants and Cafés**
see p81

2 Pak Khlong Market

MAP C5 ■ Chakphet Road ■ Open 24 hours daily

The sights, sounds, and smells at this bustling flower, fruit, and vegetable market threaten to cause sensory overload. Throughout the night, boats laden with jasmine, lotus, and carnations unload their cargo, and at dawn the colorful displays of blooms and tropical fruits are at their best. The market is at its busiest in the mornings.

Gold shops along Yaowarat Road

3 Yaowarat Road

MAP E5 ■ Shops: open 8am–10pm daily

The heart of Chinatown's gold trade, this one-way street boasts over 100 gold shops. Painted bright red, these shops flaunt glittering displays of necklaces and bracelets. The high volume of vehicles here often makes traffic come to a complete halt, and each evening the street gets even busier as foodstalls and vendors occupy every inch of space available.

4 Phahurat Market (Little India)

MAP C5 ■ Phahurat Road ■ Open 9am–6pm daily

Crossing the road in Bangkok's Chinatown can seem like traveling from China to India in the blink of an eye. An enclave within an enclave, Little India, mostly concentrated along Phahurat Road and the block to the south, shows that Indians and Chinese share a love of commerce. Saris and rainbow-colored bolts of cloth are stacked to the rooftops of the cramped shophouses and spill onto the streets. Tiny teahouses and shops selling offerings for Hindu temples complete the scene.

5 Songwat Road

MAP E6

Songwat Road runs parallel to the Chao Phraya River (see pp20–21), and though the riverside piers and wharves are less busy now than a century ago, many companies still have their warehouses in this area, especially those in the rice trade. A stroll along this road and the small lanes that lead down to the river conjures up something of the atmosphere of Chinatown in bygone days. At its western end, Songwat Road leads to Pak Khlong, the flower market.

Wat Mangkon Kamalawat, Chinatown's most revered temple

⑥ Wat Mangkon Kamalawat (Wat Leng Noi Yee)

MAP E5 ■ Charoen Krung Road ■ 02 222 3975 ■ Open 6am–6pm daily

Established in 1871, this is the most important of Chinatown's many Chinese temples. Wat Mangkon Kamalawat, or Dragon Flower Temple, is particularly active during the Vegetarian Festival in October, when devotees flock here to make offerings. Also known as Wat Leng Noi Yee, it has an impressive entrance gateway and the complex contains Buddhist, Taoist, and Confucian shrines. It is constantly busy with people making offerings, and vendors selling religious goods outside the temple do a brisk business.

YAOWARAT GOLD

The strong Chinese influence on Thai culture is evident in the love many Thais have for gold, a traditionally Chinese commodity. Thais display their status by wearing chunky bracelets and thick-linked watch straps. Gold in Bangkok is sold not by ounce but by baht, and some see it as more reliable than the country's currency.

---

⑦ Sampeng Lane

MAP L3 ■ Open 8am–8pm daily

This narrow, frenetic lane, also known as Soi Wanit 1, stretches for about half a mile (1 km) through the very heart of Chinatown and is not for the fainthearted. Cars cannot even squeeze their way down here, but motorbikes and porters carrying stacks of goods try to weave through the slow-moving sea of humanity. People pause every few steps to examine the goods on offer – from computer games, to toys and clothes.

⑧ Wat Ga Buang Kim

MAP D6 ■ Trok Krai, Anuwong Road

Set around a small, enclosed courtyard, this neighborhood temple is remarkable for its beautifully ornamented "vegetarian hall," which has an altar framed by intricately carved, gold-painted miniatures. The hall's outer wall is decorated with tableaux as well, and finely crafted ceramic figurines drawn from Chinese opera stories adorn the doorway at the top of the stairs. A second building in the temple compound functions as a stage for Chinese opera performances.

(9) Talad Kao and Talad Mai

MAP E6 ■ Soi Isara Nuphap
■ Talad Kao: open 4–11am daily;
Talad Mai: open 4am–6pm daily

These two fresh-produce markets are piled high with fish, mushrooms, mangoes, curry pastes, Chinese herbs, and spices. The Talad Kao, or Old Market, has been open for trade since the late 18th century, while the Talad Mai, or New Market, is about 100 years old. Together, they have earned themselves a good name for high-quality meat, fish, vegetables, and fruits. They remain particularly busy during the Chinese New Year. The old market is frantic at dawn, but winds down before lunchtime, while the new one continues to operate until evening.

(10) Hua Lampong Station

MAP F6 ■ Rama IV Road
■ 02 225 6964

Initiated by Rama V (see p38), Hua Lampong Station was built just before World War I by Dutch architects. Despite several revamps since then, the basic shell remains unchanged, making this train station one of Bangkok's most easily recognizable landmarks. This is the place where many out-of-towners begin their big city experience as they arrive at the railroad terminal and are more often than not preoccupied with avoiding scams rather than admiring the station's vaulted roof or mural paintings.

Monks at Hua Lampong Station

EXPLORING CHINATOWN AND LITTLE INDIA

▶ MORNING

Traffic can be a nightmare at any time in Chinatown, so take the public ferry to Tha Rachini, at around 9am. Take the first right on leaving the pier, cross the canal and go right again into **Pak Khlong Market** (see p77), which should be at its busiest and best at this time. Next, head north up Atsadang Road and then turn right into Phra Phitak Road. Within a couple of short blocks this becomes **Phahurat Road**, (see p77) and you are transported to Little India. Keep walking straight through until you reach Chak Phet Road. Have a delicious north Indian lunch at the **Royal India** (see p81) restaurant.

AFTERNOON

With your batteries recharged, plunge into **Sampeng Lane** with its kitsch gadgets and wind-up toys. Make sure that your wallet or purse is well hidden as this is a pickpocket's paradise. When you reach Soi Isara Nuphap, turn left and wander past all the Chinese herbalists and pharmacists on your way to **Yaowarat Road** (see p77). Turn right here and notice the profusion of gold shops, all painted bright red with vibrant gold lettering, and most with an armed guard on duty. Where Yaowarat Road meets Charoen Krung Road, cross to the east side of the street and enter the temple of **Wat Traimit** (see p76). Sit down for a few moments to rest and admire the superb craftsmanship of the **Golden Buddha** (see p76) and enjoy a tranquil end to the day.

See map on pp76–7

What to Buy

1 Flowers
Pak Khlong Market *(see p77)* is the place to buy fresh flowers – either individual cut blooms or a bouquet mixing a few favorites. Temperate flowers such as roses mingle with orchids and lotus ginger.

2 Gold
If you are seeking some gold ornamentation, check out the gold shops along Yaowarat Road *(see p77)*, which sell 23-carat gold in a wide variety of designs.

Freshly-cut lotus buds

3 Textiles
The fantastic range of textiles on sale in Chinatown, and particularly in Phahurat Market *(see p77)*, is enough to tempt many visitors to take home a bolt of cloth or some inexpensive ready-made garments.

Shop staff preparing packets of tea

4 Tea
Green tea and black tea, loose or packaged, is sold throughout Chinatown, and is consumed in great quantities by the Chinese themselves. Fresh markets and herbalists would be the best places for you to sniff out a good brew.

5 Incense
For the Chinese, incense is essential, particularly for making offerings, and several shops in Chinatown sell incense in coils, pyramids, small sticks, and big sticks that burn for hours.

6 Fashion Accessories
There is nothing exclusive about the cheap trinkets on sale throughout Chinatown, particularly along Sampeng Lane *(see p78)*. Plastic earrings, strings of beads, cuddly mobile phone covers, and sequined handbags are just a few of the items on offer.

7 Ceramics
Most of the ceramics on sale in Chinatown are functional rather than decorative, yet the ceramic shops are worth nosing around for unexpected treasures.

8 Lanterns
In a few of the narrow alleys off Soi Isara Nuphap some families still make traditional Chinese lanterns for a living. Shops along Sampeng Lane sell the finished product in a range of bright colors.

9 Spices
Visitors to any of the fresh markets in Chinatown can admire colorful chili pastes and spices overflowing from huge enamel basins and pick out a few to experiment with at home.

10 Temple Offerings
The most common temple offerings in Bangkok are incense and colored paper, although shops specializing in religious necessities in Chinatown also sell miniature shrines and bright robes to drape around Chinese deities.

See map on pp76–7

Restaurants and Cafés

1 Let The Boy Die
MAP M2 ▪ 542 Luang Road
▪ 09 9493 9909 ▪ Open 5pm–midnight
daily ▪ BB

Enjoy locally brewed craft beer
as well as great bistro food, such
as gourmet burgers and fish and
chips, at this popular gastropub.

2 Royal India
MAP D5 ▪ 392/1 Chak Phet
Road ▪ 02 221 6565 ▪ Open
10am–10pm daily ▪ BB

Set in a back alley, Royal India scores
low on decor, but serves diners some
great north Indian dishes.

3 Food Center, Old Siam Plaza
MAP C5 ▪ Phahurat Road ▪ Open
10am–5pm daily ▪ B

On the third floor of Old Siam Plaza,
the food court serves a good range
of Thai and Chinese dishes, while the
first floor stalls sell Thai desserts.

4 Shangarila
MAP E5 ▪ 306 Yaowarat Road
▪ 02 224 5933 ▪ Open 10:30am–10pm
daily ▪ BB

One of a chain of popular Cantonese
restaurants, this huge place serves
great fare, including *dim sum*, soups,
and stir-fries.

Delicious fare at Shangarila

PRICE CATEGORIES
For a meal for one with one or two dishes
and a soft drink, including service.

B under B200   BB B200–1,000
BBB over B1,000

5 Hua Seng Hong
MAP E5 ▪ 371 Yaowarat Road
▪ 02 222 7053 ▪ Open 9–1am daily
▪ BB

Famed for its tasty bird's nest soup,
Hua Seng Hong also offers dishes
such as *hoy tawt* (mussels in batter).

6 T & K
MAP E6 ▪ 49 Soi Phadungdao
▪ 02 223 4519 ▪ Open 4:30pm–2am
daily ▪ BB

A busy Chinatown restaurant, T & K
specializes in barbecued seafood.

7 Hong Kong Noodles
MAP E5 ▪ 136/4 Soi Charoen
Krung 16 ▪ Open 10am–8pm daily
▪ B

This is a bustling, popular restaurant
specializing in roast duck noodles.

8 Chong Kee
MAP F6 ▪ 84 Soi Sukon 1,
Trimit Road ▪ Open 9:30am–2pm
Mon, 9:30am–5:30pm Tue–Sun ▪ B

Customers flock here for the house
specialty – pork satay on sweet toast.

9 Tep Bar
MAP M3 ▪ Soi Nana (near
Charoen Krung Road) ▪ (09) 8467
2944 ▪ Open 5pm–midnight Sun–
Thu, 5pm–1am Fri & Sat ▪ BB

On artsy Soi Nana, Tep offers
delicious food including grilled
meats and spicy salads. Also try
their Thai herbal whiskey.

10 Ba Hao
MAP M3 ▪ 8 Soi Nana (near
Charoen Krung Road) ▪ 06 4635 1989
▪ Open 6pm–midnight Tue–Sun ▪ BB

Tuck into Chinese comfort food, teas,
ginseng shots, and cocktails at this
chic Chinoiserie.

TOP 10 Downtown

Bangkok's Downtown area radiates out eastward from the Old City and Chinatown. This densely built-up area includes embassies and offices as well as top hotels, restaurants, and entertainment venues. There are a few historical sights, including the Assumption Cathedral, and some gorgeous traditional houses that contrast with all the surrounding skyscrapers. Lush Lumphini Park provides an escape from the concrete jungle, while Silom Road, Siam Square, and Ploenchit are the best shopping areas. Silom is also one of the city's liveliest areas for nightlife; along its infamous side streets, Patpong 1 and 2, market stalls and bars featuring live bands compete with go-go bars for visitors' attention.

Prehistoric pottery, Suan Pakkad

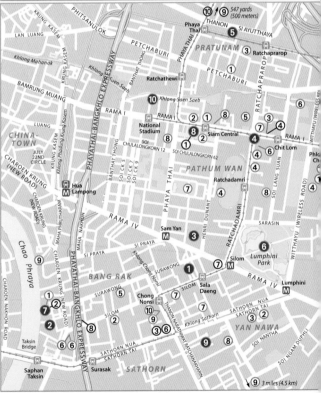

DOWNTOWN

1 Patpong

MAP P5 ■ Between Silom and Surawong roads ■ Markets and bars open 6pm–1am daily

Named after a Chinese millionaire who first started to develop these narrow lanes, Patpong 1 and 2 became world famous when their go-go bars were visited by US soldiers on leave from Vietnam in the late 1960s. Its heyday was in the 1980s, during Thailand's first tourist boom. In the early 1990s, a night market was set up along the length of Patpong 1, and the raunchy nightlife began to decline. The downstairs bars include live music cafés and loud go-go bars. Exercise caution at these places, and note that many upstairs bars are rip-off joints.

The elaborate Assumption Cathedral

2 Assumption Cathedral

MAP M6 ■ Soi Oriental ■ 02 234 8556 ■ Open 6am–7pm daily

In quiet backstreets near the river, this imposing building, erected in 1910, replaced a structure from the 1820s. It dominates a tree-lined square that is part of a Catholic mission. The elaborate pink and white exterior matches the bright Rococo interior. The cathedral bears testimony to the success of French missions to Bangkok in the 19th century. While they made few conversions, they managed to secure religious tolerance for all.

3 The Queen Saovabha Memorial Institute

MAP P4 ■ 1871 Rama IV Road ■ 02 252 0161 ■ Shows: 2:30pm Mon–Fri, 11am Sat–Sun ■ Adm

One of Bangkok's quirkier sights, Queen Saovabha Memorial Institute (see p50) was set up in 1923 as the Pasteur Institute. The Thai Red Cross runs it now, producing serums for snake bites and promoting education about snakes. During live demonstrations, snakes are milked of their venom.

1 **Top 10 Sights**
see pp84–7

1 **Restaurants**
see p91

1 **Best of the Rest**
see p88

1 **Bars and Pubs**
see p92

1 **Shopping Malls**
see p89

1 **Nightclubs and Music Venues**
see p93

SIRAT EXPRESSWAY

Makkasan

PETCHABURI

SUKHUMVIT SOI 3

Nana

ASOK MONTRI

Sukhumvit

BTS Asok

SUKHUMVIT ROAD

RATCHADAPHISEK ROAD

Benchakitti Park

Benchasiri Park

SUKHUMVIT SOI 22

SUKHUMVIT SOI 24

MAHANAKHON EXPY

Khlong Toei

Queen Sirikit National Convention Centre

RAMA IV

0 meters 1000
0 yards 1000

4 Erawan Shrine

MAP Q3 ■ **Corner of Ratchadamri and Ploenchit roads**

An island of spirituality in a sea of commerce, the Erawan Shrine is one of Bangkok's quirkiest sights, with the Skytrain zipping by and shopping malls hemming it in. Thailand's most famous spirit house gained its fame in 1956 when its installation was credited with halting a string of fatal accidents at the construction site of the former Erawan Hotel. A constant stream of suppliants offer marigolds, incense, and candles, along with silent wishes.

Erawan Shrine

5 Suan Pakkad

MAP Q1 ■ **352–354 Si Ayutthaya Road** ■ **02 246 1775–6** ■ **Open 9am–4pm daily** ■ **Adm** ■ **www. suanpakkad.com/main_eng.php**

This compound of traditional houses was assembled in the 1950s by Prince and Princess Chumbhot on former farmland (the name means "cabbage patch"). The museum has a varied collection of statues, paintings, porcelain, *khon* theater masks, and musical instruments.

6 Lumphini Park

MAP Q4 ■ **Corner of Ratchadamri and Rama IV roads** ■ **Open 5am–8pm daily**

It is difficult to imagine how Bangkok might be without this green lung that occupies a huge block in the heart of the commercial and entertainment district. Consisting of a large lake, well-tended lawns, and shady trees, it is busy from dawn with locals walking, jogging, and performing t'ai chi in groups. From February to April, it is a popular site for kite-flying.

7 Oriental Hotel

MAP M5 ■ **48 Oriental Avenue** ■ **02 659 9000** ■ **www.mandarinoriental. com/bangkok**

Bangkok's oldest hotel enjoys double billing as both historic sight and luxurious accommodation option. It has hosted several famous writers, including Joseph Conrad and Somerset Maugham, in the Authors' Wing. Built in 1876, this original part of the hotel is now dwarfed by the Garden and River Wings, but still attracts visitors for afternoon tea in its Authors' Lounge.

8 Siam Square

MAP P2 ■ **Corner of Rama I and Phaya Thai roads**

Flanked by multistory malls, Siam Square is a grid of streets packed with shopping arcades. The numerous tiny shops, some with no more than a meter frontage, make it a popular shopping area, especially for students from the neighboring Chulalongkorn University, who congregate around Center Point's milk bars and fast-food outlets at the southern end of the square. There are also shops selling designer clothes and fashion accessories, the creation of enterprising young Thai designers, plus a good selection of cafés, restaurants, and cinemas.

The lake at Lumphini Park

M. R. Kukrit's serene home

9 M. R. Kukrit's Heritage Home

MAP P6 ■ Soi 7, Narathiwat Ratchanakarin Road ■ 02 286 8185 ■ Open 10am–4pm daily ■ Adm

Descended from Rama II *(see p31)*, Mom Rajawongse Kukrit Pramoj (1911–95) was one of the best-loved Thais of the 20th century. He founded the newspaper *Siam Rath* and wrote hundreds of plays, poems, and novels. He even served as Prime Minister in 1975–6. His house, with many beautiful artworks and a garden, is preserved as he left it.

BANGKOK TRAFFIC

Traffic in Bangkok is known for going nowhere. Drivers sit in a sea of vehicles. Yet it was not always like this. In *The Land of the White Elephant* (1873), Frank Vincent writes: "the nobles...may occasionally be seen taking a drive at the fashionable hour of the afternoon, sitting gravely upright and...looking upon their friends...with a sense of new-found importance."

10 Jim Thompson House

One of the most popular sights in Bangkok, this beautiful compound of traditional Thai houses *(see pp28–9)* set in a lush tropical garden allows visitors to imagine how life in a well-to-do, mid-20th century Bangkok home might have been. The evocative furnishings, sculptures, and tapestries give the building a refined character. Visitors to the house must join a guided tour, which are regular and in several languages.

A WALK THROUGH THE OLD FARANG QUARTER

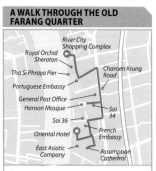

MORNING

Begin this half-mile (1-km) walking tour at the upscale **River City Shopping Complex**, on the riverfront just north of the pier at Tha Si Phraya. You will find jewelry, books, restaurants, clothes, and more. On the third and fourth floor are shops selling rare antiques, and an antiques auction is held every second month. From here head back south, passing the **Royal Orchid Sheraton** *(see p114)* to glimpse the **Portuguese Embassy**. Operational from 1820, this was the first embassy to be established in Siam by any European power. Follow the lane out to Charoen Krung Road and turn right to reach the **General Post Office**, a massive Art Deco building. Walk south along Charoen Krung from the post office and turn right into Soi 34 to see old wooden houses; the winding lane leads to **Haroon Mosque**, a small, attractive stucco building used by the local Muslim population. The next lane south, Soi 36, is home to the **French Embassy**, which was the second embassy to be established in Bangkok. Walk south, crossing Soi 38 and 40 to reach the **Assumption Cathedral** *(see p85)*. From the cathedral, follow an alley west towards the river, where the former headquarters of the East Asiatic Company, built in 1901, still stands. Have tea and cakes in the Authors' Lounge at the historic **Oriental Hotel** next door to end your morning's walk.

See map on pp84–5

The Best of the Rest

1 Pratunam Market

MAP Q1 ■ Corner of Phetburi and Ratchaprarop roads ■ Open 9am–midnight daily

Famous for its inexpensive textiles and ready-made clothes, Pratunam Market is a great place to witness the city's chaotic street life.

2 Maha Uma Devi Temple

MAP N5 ■ Corner of Silom Road and Soi Pan ■ 02 238 4007 ■ Open 6am–8pm daily

Also known as Sri Mariamman, this temple features a panoply of brightly painted Hindu deities above the entrance and around the interior walls.

Statue at Maha Uma Devi

3 Baiyoke Sky Hotel

MAP Q1 ■ 222 Ratchaprarop Road ■ 02 656 3000 ■ Open 10–2am daily ■ Adm

Bangkok's second-tallest building at 1,000 ft (304 m), this tower has an open-air, revolving roof deck that offers superb panoramas of the city.

4 Royal Bangkok Sports Club

MAP Q3 ■ Henri Dunant Road ■ 02 652 5000 ■ www.rbsc.org

This attractive horse-racing club has a golf course set inside the track.

5 Neilson Hays Library

MAP N5 ■ 195 Suriwong Road ■ 02 233 1731 ■ Open 9:30am–5pm Tue–Sun

Located in a colonial building, this haven for bookworms has over 20,000 volumes on its shelves.

6 Chao Mae Tubtim Shrine

MAP R2 ■ Wireless Road

This eye-catching shrine (see p52) is encircled by phallic offerings from devotees wishing for fertility or prosperity.

7 Chulalongkorn University

MAP P3 ■ Phaya Thai Road ■ 02 215 0871 ■ www.chula.ac.th

The campus of Thailand's oldest and most respected university mixes Western and Thai architectural styles.

8 SEA LIFE Bangkok Ocean World

MAP P2 ■ Basement, Siam Paragon, Rama I Road ■ 02 687 2000 ■ Open 10am–9pm daily ■ Adm ■ www.sealifebangkok.com

This aquarium (see p51), home to over 400 species of marine life, features an underwater tunnel.

9 Museum of Counterfeit Goods

MAP T6 ■ Tilleke & Gibbins, Supalai Grand Tower, Rama III Road ■ 02 056 5548 ■ Open by appointment

Quirky displays of over 4,000 fake items, including clothing and drugs.

10 King Power Mahanakhon

MAP P5 ■ Narathiwat Ratchanakharin Road ■ Open 10am–midnight daily ■ Adm

Currently Thailand's tallest building, this place has an observation deck at 1,030 ft (314 m).

King Power Mahanakhon

Shopping Malls

1 Siam Paragon
MAP P2 ▪ Rama I Road, Siam Square ▪ 02 610 8000 ▪ Open 10am–10pm daily ▪ www.siamparagon.co.th

With six floors of designer boutiques, bookshops, cinemas, restaurants, and fitness centers, this mall is one of the most popular in Bangkok.

2 Siam Center and Siam Discovery Center
MAP P2 ▪ Rama I Road ▪ 02 658 1000 ▪ Open 10am–10pm daily

Known for designer brands, trendy shops, and restaurants, these two adjoining malls attract young adults. Look out for local fashion labels such as Greyhound, Baking Soda, and Theatre.

3 Narai Phand
MAP Q2 ▪ President Tower, 973 Ploenchit Road ▪ 02 656 0398 ▪ Open 10am–8pm daily

At this government-sponsored shop for promoting quality Thai handi-crafts, everything is sold at fixed prices: woodcarvings, lacquerware, silk clothing, silverware, and more.

4 Peninsula Plaza
MAP Q3 ▪ 153 Ratchadamri Road ▪ 02 254 3320 ▪ Open 10am–8pm daily

This mall consists mostly of jewelers and designer outlets.

5 Central World
MAP Q2 ▪ 4/1–2 Ratchadamri Road ▪ 02 640 7000 ▪ Open 10am–10pm daily ▪ www.centralworld.co.th

Huge shopping complex (see p60) with fashion boutiques, home decor outlets, a bowling alley, and cinemas.

6 Erawan Bangkok
MAP Q3 ▪ 494 Ploenchit Road ▪ 02 250 7777 ▪ Open 10am–9pm daily ▪ www.erawanbangkok.com

Next to the Erawan Shrine, this luxury mall has plenty of boutiques by famous names, as well as classy cafés and a wellness center.

The stylish Gaysorn Village

7 Gaysorn Village
MAP Q2 ▪ Ploenchit Road ▪ 02 656 1149 ▪ Open 10am–10pm daily

International luxury brands and a few local designer stores display their wares here.

8 Mahboonkrong (MBK)
MAP P3 ▪ Phaya Thai Road ▪ Open 10am–10pm daily ▪ www.mbk-center.co.th

Packed with seven floors of fashions, accessories, electronics, cosmetics, jewelry, and eateries, MBK (see p60) feels like a cross between a street market and a shopping mall.

9 EmQuartier
MAP T6 ▪ 693 Sukhumvit Road ▪ 02 269 1188 ▪ Open 10am–10pm daily ▪ www.emporium.co.th

Across the street from the Emporium (see p61), this mall has a less formal atmosphere and many boutiques.

10 Emporium
MAP T6 ▪ 622 Sukhumvit Road ▪ 02 269 1000 ▪ Open 10am–10pm daily ▪ www.emporium.co.th

An upscale mall, Emporium (see p61) features a department store, designer boutiques, restaurants, and cafés.

See map on pp84–5

Ways to Enjoy the River

① Chao Phraya Express Boats

www.chaophrayaexpressboat.com
This extensive public transport system is both picturesque and useful. There are several color-coded routes, and the website explains everything.

② Loy Nava Cruise

MAP M5 ■ Si Phraya Pier ■ 02 437 4932 ■ Cruise 6–8pm & 8:10–10:10pm ■ www.loynava.com ■ BBB

Choose from traditional, seafood, and vegetarian Thai dishes, then sit back and enjoy the fare on this rice barge as it chugs up and down the Chao Phraya River.

③ Anantara Sleep-on-Board Cruise to Ayutthaya

bangkok-cruises.anantara.com
The Anantara hotel group offers luxurious three-day cruises up the Chao Phraya to Ayutthaya, with accommodation aboard their lavishly refurbished teak rice barges. Although this is an expensive trip, it is a memorable experience.

Anantara sleep-on-board cruise

④ Canal Tours

These can be arranged with a tour agency or by negotiating with the boat captains directly. Good stops are the Royal Barge Museum (see p96) and the artist's house at Khlong Bang Luang (see p62).

⑤ Hotel and Other Free Shuttles

Just west of the BTS Saphan Taksin station, take a shuttle voyage to one of the spectacular riverside hotels on the Thonburi bank – such as the Millennium Hilton or the Anantara – for a meal or drink.

⑥ Charter Long-Tail Boat to Koh Kret

At any riverside pier, enterprising long-tail boat captains offer their vessels for hire. If you have a group of four or more, a visit to Koh Kret (see p95) would make for an excellent day trip. Agree a price, and pay upon returning to your point of origin.

⑦ Manohra Cruise

MAP S6 ■ Anantara Bangkok Riverside Pier ■ 02 476 0022 ■ Cruise 7:30–9:30pm ■ www.manohra cruises.com ■ BBB

Operating out of the Anantara Bangkok Riverside, this cruise offers guests tasty curries and stir-fries.

⑧ Grand Pearl Cruise

MAP M5 ■ River City Pier ■ 02 861 0255 ■ Cruise 7:30–9:30pm ■ www.grandpearlcruise.com ■ BBB

This cruise is perfect for those looking for a lively evening. Boats are big and offer live music and lounge areas, plus a blowout buffet.

⑨ Taking the Boat to Bang Krajao

This oasis of clean air and greenery (see p97) can be reached by a public boat from behind Wat Khlong Toey Nok or by chartering a private long-tail from anywhere on the river.

⑩ Yok Yor Cruise

MAP L4 ■ Soi 20, Tha Din Daeng Road, Thonburi ■ 02 863 0565 ■ Cruise 8–10pm ■ www.yokyor.co.th/english ■ BB

Bangkok's only budget dinner cruise is popular but the menu is limited.

Restaurants

1 Le Normandie

MAP M5 ■ Mandarin Oriental Hotel, 48 Oriental Avenue ■ 02 659 9000 ■ Open noon–2pm & 7–10pm Mon–Sat ■ www.mandarinoriental.com/bangkok ■ BBB

The Brittany lobster and pan-fried duck liver are specialties of this French restaurant (see p59).

2 Ban Khun Mae

MAP P2 ■ 458/7–9 Siam Square Soi 8 ■ 02 250 1952 ■ Open 11am–11pm daily ■ BB

With its extensive menu of classic Thai dishes, Ban Khun Mae is an ideal spot for lunch or dinner.

3 Rang Mahal

MAP T6 ■ Rembrandt Hotel, 26th floor, Sukhumvit Soi 18 ■ 02 261 7050 ■ Open 5pm–midnight daily & 11am–2:30pm Sun ■ BB

Consistently named Bangkok's best Indian restaurant, Rang Mahal (see p59) serves elegant, authentic Northern Indian cuisine and has great views.

4 Liu

MAP R3 ■ Conrad Hotel, 87 Wireless Road ■ 02 690 9999 ■ Open 11:30am–2:30pm & 6–10:30pm daily ■ BB

This gourmet Chinese restaurant (see p59) serves classic regional cuisines – Cantonese, Shanghainese, Sichuan – with a contemporary twist.

5 Lenzi Tuscan Kitchen

MAP Q3 ■ Ruam Rudee Soi 2 ■ 02 001 0116 ■ Open 11:45am–2pm & 6–10:45pm daily ■ BB

Famous for several Italian restaurants, the chef focuses on native Tuscany dishes here (see p59). Produce comes from the family farm near Pisa.

6 Breeze

MAP M6 ■ 52nd floor, State Tower, 1055 Silom Road ■ 02 624 9555 ■ Open 6–11pm daily ■ BBB

Come here for spectacular views and impeccable (but pricey) Asian food.

Incredible food and views at Breeze

7 Eat Me

MAP P5 ■ Soi Pipat 2, Convent Road ■ 02 238 0931 ■ Open 3pm–1am daily ■ BB

A very imaginative international fusion menu is offered here (see p59).

8 Gaggan

MAP Q3 ■ 68/1 Soi Langsuan (opp Soi 3) ■ 02 652 1700 ■ Sittings at 5:30 & 9:30pm Mon–Sat ■ BBB

Gaggan (see p59) serves progressive Indian food.

9 L'Atelier de Joël Robuchon

MAP P5 ■ MahaNakhon CUBE, 5th floor, Narathiwat Ratchanakarin Road ■ 02 001 0698 ■ Open 11:30am–2pm & 6:30–10pm daily ■ BBB

French haute cuisine is served in an informal setting. Robuchon has been called "chef of the century."

10 Issaya Siamese Club

MAP off R6 ■ 4 Soi Sri Aksorn, Chua Ploeng Road ■ 02 672 9040–1 ■ Open 11:30am–3pm & 6–10:30pm daily ■ BB

Housed in a mansion, this restaurant (see p59) serves Thai cuisine.

See map on pp84–5

Bars and Pubs

① Diplomat Bar
MAP R3 ▪ Conrad Hotel, All Seasons Place, 87 Wireless Road (Witthayu) ▪ 02 690 9244 ▪ Open 7am–1am Sun–Thu, 7am–2am Fri & Sat

Unwind along with the high-flyers at this super-elegant bar while sipping a cocktail and enjoying the resident jazz band.

② The Zuk Bar
MAP Q5 ▪ Sukhothai Hotel, 13/3 South Sathorn Road ▪ 02 344 8888 ▪ Open 5pm–1am Mon–Sat, 5pm–midnight Sun ▪ www.sukho thai.com

Surrounded by gardens and lotus ponds, the bar at this elegant, low-rise hotel is a relaxing place for drinks at the end of a hot day, accompanied by Spanish hams, cheese platters and other tapas.

③ Moon Bar
MAP Q6 ▪ Banyan Tree Hotel, South Sathorn Road ▪ 02 679 1200 ▪ Open 5pm–1am daily

Enjoy the fabulous views from high up above the city at Moon Bar, which offers a complete range of cocktails.

Spectacular views from Moon Bar

④ Bar@494
MAP Q3 ▪ 494 Ratchadamri Road ▪ 02 254 6250 ▪ Open 3pm–midnight daily

The excellent wines and tapas are reasonably priced at this small bar in the Grand Hyatt Erawan.

⑤ Oskar Bistro
MAP T6 ▪ 24 Sukhumvit Soi 11 ▪ 09 7289 4410 ▪ Open 4pm–2am daily

Great for a pre- or post-clubbing drink and snack, this stylish place has good craft beers and cocktails.

⑥ Sky Bar
MAP M6 ▪ 63rd floor, State Tower, 1055 Silom Road ▪ 02 624 9555 ▪ Open 6pm–1am daily

Indulge in a pricey sundowner at the Sky Bar and admire the view.

⑦ Namsaah Bottling Trust
MAP P5 ▪ Soi 7, Silom Road ▪ 02 636 6622 ▪ Open 5pm–1am daily

This retro-kitsch gastrobar in a bright pink, 100-year-old villa serves creative cocktails and great fusion food.

⑧ Small's
MAP Q6 ▪ 186/3 Suan Phlu Soi 1 ▪ 09 5585 1398 ▪ Open 7:30pm–2am Wed–Mon

Come here for the city's best whiskey selection. Light meals are served while jazz plays in the background.

⑨ Viva & Aviv The River
MAP M5 ▪ Ground floor, River City shopping centre ▪ 02 639 6305 ▪ Open 10–1am daily

Wonderful cocktails, comfort food and a lovely river terrace are high-lights of this riverside bar.

⑩ Hyde and Seek
MAP R3 ▪ Athenée Residence, 65/1 Soi Ruam Rudee ▪ 02 168 5152 ▪ Open 11:30am–2pm & 5:30–10pm daily

This classy but lively gastrobar, has an appealing garden seating, and features DJs every night.

Nightclubs and Music Venues

The popular Hard Rock Café

1 Hard Rock Café
MAP P3 ■ 424/3–6 Soi 11, Siam Square ■ 02 658 4090 ■ Open 11am–midnight daily

Popular worldwide, this is one of the city's liveliest night spots.

2 Bamboo Bar
MAP M5 ■ Oriental Hotel, 48 Oriental Avenue ■ 02 659 9000 ■ Open 5pm–1:30am Fri & Sat (until 12:30am Sun–Thu ■ www.mandarinoriental.com/bangkok

With an excellent resident band this is a brilliant spot *(see p56)* for jazz lovers.

3 WOOBAR®
MAP P6 ■ W Bangkok Hotel, 106 North Sathorn Road ■ 02 344 4131 ■ Open 9am–midnight daily

A variety of sounds, from techno to funky house, are played at this beautifully sophisticated hotel bar.

4 Mixx Discotheque
MAP Q2 ■ President Tower Arcade, 973 Phloen Chit Road ■ 02 656 0383 ■ Open 10pm–2am daily ■ Adm

Known for its superb acoustics and sound system, this club plays hip-hop, R&B, and house music.

5 Levels
MAP T6 ■ Aloft Hotel, 6th floor, Sukhumvit Soi 11 ■ (08) 2308 3246 ■ Open 9pm–3am daily

Different styles of music play in each of this hot club's three party zones, which include a chill-out lounge bar.

6 The Club @ Koi
MAP N6 ■ Sathorn Square Complex, 98 North Sathorn Road ■ 02 108 2005 ■ Open 6pm–2am Tue–Sat ■ Adm on weekends

Downtown's most elegant dancing spot occupies the two top floors of a skyscraper. The music varies nightly.

7 DJ Station
MAP P5 ■ Silom Soi 2 ■ 02 266 4029 ■ Open 9:30pm–2am daily ■ Adm

Silom Soi 2 is dominated by gay clubs, and this three-floor nightclub is the most popular.

8 Maggie Choo's
MAP M5 ■ Novotel Bangkok Fenix Silom Hotel, 320 Silom Road ■ 091 772 2144 ■ Open 6pm–3am daily

One of Bangkok's most imaginative nightspots, this has 1930s decor, live jazz, and good food on offer.

Jazz band at Maggie Choo's

9 Saxophone
MAP T6 ■ 3/8 Phaya Thai Road ■ 02 246 5472 ■ Open 6pm–2am daily

A Bangkok music institution for 30 years, Saxophone offers live jazz, blues, and reggae. It's a friendly spot that is also popular with locals for its excellent Thai food.

10 Raintree
MAP T6 ■ Soi Ruamjit, Rangnam Road ■ 02 245 7230 ■ Open 5pm–1:30am daily

An authentic Thai night out: folk rock, pop bands, and spicy food.

See map on pp84–5

TOP 10 Greater Bangkok

Most of Bangkok's suburban areas are housing estates, but there are also some unmissable sights, like Chatuchak Weekend Market. The former capital Thonburi has the enigmatic Wat Arun and the Royal Barge Museum. To the north of the Old City, Dusit features Wat Benjamabophit. East of the center lie Kamthieng House and the Rama IX Royal Park, while a short boat ride north, Nonthaburi and Koh Kret offer a taste of provincial Thailand.

Riverside Wat Arun

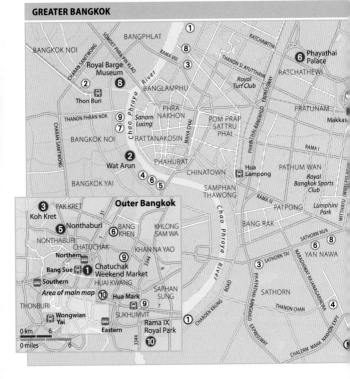

GREATER BANGKOK

1 Chatuchak Weekend Market

This market (see pp26–7) covers a massive area, with about 15,000 stalls selling a mind-boggling range of products, from plants and animals to antiques and paintings. Considered to be the world's largest open-air market, Chatuchak is too big to see everything in a day, so pick up a map at the entrance and target the areas that interest you.

2 Wat Arun

This ancient temple (see pp30–31) in Thonburi, on the west bank of the Chao Phraya River (see pp20–21), is one of Bangkok's best-known icons with its five *prangs* (towers). These *prangs* are covered with broken shards of colorful porcelain that create an intriguing abstract pattern when viewed up close. The temple's *bot* (ordination hall) is also worth exploring, both for its murals and the exquisite Buddha image, which was apparently molded by King Rama II.

3 Koh Kret
MAP S4 ■ 4 miles (7 km) N of Nonthaburi

Combining a trip to Nonthaburi (see p96) with an exploration of Koh Kret, an ox-bow island in a meander of the Chao Phraya River (see pp20–21), makes for an enjoyable day. Hire a longtail boat from Nonthaburi to reach Koh Kret. The island is inhabited by the Mon people, who make terra-cotta pots for sale in markets in the city. There are no cars, so you can listen to the twitter of birds as you wander around the island, passing mango, papaya, and durian plantations, pausing to watch busy potters at work, and perhaps picking up a sample of their work.

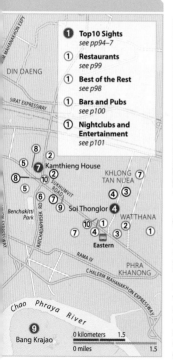

1	**Top10 Sights** see pp94–7
1	**Restaurants** see p99
1	**Best of the Rest** see p98
1	**Bars and Pubs** see p100
1	**Nightclubs and Entertainment** see p101

Temple on the island of Koh Kret

4 Soi Thonglor
MAP T6

Also known as Sukhumvit Soi 55, this area of east Bangkok is popular with young Thai professionals and expats. There's nothing of great cultural significance here, but the area has a fun vibe, with many restaurants, bars, and boutiques. Take BTS to Thonglor station, stroll a mile (1.6 km) up one side of the street and return on the other, taking in the lively cafés and entertainment venues.

Fruit and vegetable vendors spread out their produce in Nonthaburi market

5 Nonthaburi
MAP S4 ▪ Nonthaburi Province

Take the express boat heading upstream from any pier in the city center and get off at the last stop in Nonthaburi. Here, the Wat Chalerm Phra Kiet temple, originally built by Rama III *(see p31)*, features intricate porcelain tilework on the doors and window frames of the *bot* (ordination hall). This region is famed for the superior quality of its durian fruit.

Phayathai Palace's cone-topped turret

6 Phayathai Palace
**MAP H1 ▪ Ratchawithi Road
▪ 02 354 7987 ▪ Tours 1pm Tue & Thu,
9:30am and 1:30pm Sat & Sun**

This palace was built in 1909 as a royal country retreat. After the 1932 coup *(see p38)*, it was commandeered by the Thai military as a hospital (Phramongkutklao Hospital), which still functions around the palace today. The highlight of the palace is the Thewaratsaparom Throne Hall, which has beautifully carved pillars, balconies, and archways.

7 Kamthieng House
MAP T6 ▪ 131 Sukhumvit Soi 21 ▪ 02 661 6470–3 ▪ Open 9am–5pm Tue–Sat ▪ www.siam-society.org

This beautiful Lanna house began life in the mid-19th century as the home of the Nimman-heimin family in Chiang Mai, but was carefully dismantled and reconstructed on this site in 1962 when it was donated to the Siam Society. Today it functions as an ethnological museum, with farming implements, a multi-media display on the Thai belief in spirits, a rural kitchen, and a granary with an exhibition on rice-farming rituals.

8 Royal Barge Museum
MAP A2 ▪ Khlong Bangkok Noi ▪ 02 424 0004 ▪ Open 9am–5pm daily ▪ Adm

This display of vessels offers a glimpse into the pageantry of the Thai monarchy. On rare ceremonial occasions, the elaborately decorated barges are propelled by bedecked oarsmen. The main barge on display, *Suphannahongse*, carries the Thai King and Queen at such times. It is carved out of a single teak tree. Its prow is adorned with a majestic golden swan.

9 Bang Krajao
MAP T6 ■ MRT to Khlong
Toey, then taxi to pier behind
Wat Khlong Toey Nok

Cycling is a great way to see this
area, an oasis of traditional villages,
mangrove forests, and fruit orchards
on the west side of the Chao Phraya
River. Bicycles can be hired at the pier.
Nearby, the Sri Nakhon Kuenkhan
Park has huge trees, landscaped
gardens, and pavilions on a lake.

THE DREADED DURIAN
The durian, a most unusual fruit,
arouses adoration and disgust in
equal measure for its strong repelling
smell and heavenly creamy taste.
The spiky shell belies the soft yellow
pods beneath it, cushioned by thick
padding. The mushy texture and
smooth, tangy taste take some
getting used to, but once hooked
there is no going back.

10 Rama IX Royal Park
MAP U6 ■ Sukhumvit Soi 103
■ Open 5am–7pm daily ■ Adm

This is an ideal spot to head
for when you need a break from
Bangkok's relentless congestion.
Though it takes a while to get to
the park, on entering the sprawling
site, the effort becomes worthwhile.
The park was opened in 1987 to
commemorate the 60th birthday
of Rama IX *(see p39)*, and contains
a museum explaining the life and
achievements of the king, a large
lake with pedal boats, as well as
beautifully landscaped grounds with
several unusual
plants that are
clearly labeled.

**Rama IX
Royal Park**

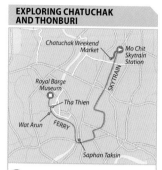

EXPLORING CHATUCHAK AND THONBURI

▶ **MORNING**

Start before 8am and make your
way to Mo Chit Skytrain station
for a good look round **Chatuchak
Weekend Market** *(see pp26–7)*. Pick
up a map at the main entrance on
the Phaholyothin Road and go
straight ahead through the maze
of stalls to the slender clocktower
to orient yourself. Check out section 8 (handicrafts), wander through
sections 9–15 (pets and accessories)
before stocking up your wardrobe
in sections 10–21 (clothing and
footwear). As there are thousands
of foodstalls, you can refuel when-
ever you get hungry or thirsty.

AFTERNOON

At midday, return to Mo Chit Skytrain
Station and take the Skytrain to
Saphan Taksin. From here, take
an express boat upriver to Tha
Tien, then hop on one of the regular cross-river ferries to **Wat
Arun** *(see pp30–31)*. Take a good
look at the bright ceramics on
the *prangs* (towers), and clamber
up the steep steps of the central
spire for a panoramic river view.
Rest in a breezy riverside pavilion before taking the ferry back
to Tha Tien. Get some refreshment at **Supanniga** *(see p75)*,
just around the corner, then take
an express boat to Phra Pinklao
pier, which is a ten-minute walk
from the **Royal Barge Museum**
(see p21): head up the road and
take the first left down Soi Wat
Dusitaram. Marvel over the
intricate decoration of the other-
worldly vessels on display here
before heading back to your base.

See map on pp94–5 ←

The Best of the Rest

 Christian Churches
MAP S5 ■ S of Ratchawithi Road

Near the riverbank in Dusit district are three churches built for resident foreigners: St. Francis Xavier Church with its mainly Vietnamese congregation, the Church of the Immaculate Conception, which was established by French missionaries, and a small Cambodian church.

Mural at Wat Suwannaram

 Wat Suwannaram
MAP S5 ■ 33 Soi 32, Charan Sanit Wong Road ■ 02 433 8045 ■ Open 8am–5pm daily

This temple is home to superb murals depicting episodes from the *Jataka* tales, which tell the story of the Buddha's previous lives.

Wat Indrawiharn
MAP D1 ■ 144 Wisut Kasat Road ■ 02 281 1406 ■ Open 6am–6pm daily

The main attraction of this temple tucked away in the backstreets of Dusit is the 105-ft (32-m) tall standing Buddha.

 Wat Kalayanamit
MAP B6 ■ Soi 6, Arun Amarin Road ■ Open 8am–5pm daily

The country's largest indoor sitting Buddha (50 ft/15 m) and its biggest bronze bell are both found here.

Wat Prayun
MAP C6 ■ Pratchatipok Road ■ Open 8am–6pm daily

An artificial hill covered with *chedis* (stupas) and shrines is the highlight at Wat Prayun's cemetery. Devotees release turtles in the pond nearby.

Church of Santa Cruz
MAP C6 ■ Soi Kudi Chin ■ Open 5–8pm Mon–Sat & 9am–8pm Sun

Established by the Portuguese in 1770, this church's building dates back to 1913. It is now pastel in color and has an octagonal dome.

Wat Rakhang
MAP A4 ■ Soi Wat Rakhang

This temple has a wooden scripture library behind the *bot* (ordination hall), where there are murals from the days when Rama I (r.1782–1809) lived here as a monk.

Thewet Flower Market
MAP D1 ■ Krung Kasem Road ■ Open 9am–6pm daily

With its bright blooms, sweet scent in the air, and the friendly vendors, this canalside market is good to explore.

Prasart Museum
MAP U6 ■ 9 Krungthep Kreetha Soi 4A ■ 02 379 3601 ■ Open 9:30am–2pm Tue–Sun (by appointment) ■ Adm

Set in a landscaped garden, this museum features artworks housed in reproductions of famous buildings.

Bangkok Dolls Museum
MAP T5 ■ 85 Soi Mo Leng, Ratchaprarop Road ■ 02 245 3008 ■ Open 8am–5pm Tue–Sat ■ www.bangkokdolls.com

This museum (see p51) displays dolls from around the world.

Restaurants

PRICE CATEGORIES

For a meal for one with one or two dishes and a soft drink, including service.

B under B200 **BB** B200–1,000
BBB over B1,000

① Bo.Lan

MAP T6 ■ 24 Sukhumvit Soi 53 ■ 02 260 2962 ■ Open 6–10:30pm Tue–Sun, noon–2pm Sat & Sun ■ BBB

Set in a beautiful wooden house near Soi Thonglor, Bo.Lan serves authentic but unusual Thai cuisine.

② Le Dalat

MAP T6 ■ 57 Sukhumvit Soi 23 (Soi Prasanmitr) ■ 02 259 9593 ■ Open 11:30am–2:30pm & 5:30–10pm daily ■ BB

Bangkok's top Vietnamese restaurant serves diners a host of exquisitely prepared traditional dishes.

③ Blue Elephant

MAP N6 ■ 233 South Sathorn Road ■ 02 673 9353–8 ■ Open 11:30am–2:30pm & 6–10:30pm daily ■ www.blueelephant.com ■ BBB

Set in a stunning century-old building, the Blue Elephant specializes in Royal Thai cuisine.

④ Rendez-vous au Lys

MAP T6 ■ 148/11 Nang Linchi Soi 6 ■ 02 077 5453 ■ Open 11am–2:30pm & 5:30–11pm Mon, Tue, & Thu–Sat, 11am–11pm Sun ■ BB

This garden restaurant serves traditional French cuisine, including good-value set lunches.

Thai food at Celadon

⑤ Cabbages & Condoms

MAP T6 ■ 10 Sukhumvit Soi 12 ■ 02 229 4610 ■ Open 11am–10:30pm daily ■ BB

Reasonable prices make this place a good choice, and all proceeds go toward AIDS prevention programs.

⑥ Baan Khanitha

MAP T6 ■ 69 South Sathorn Road ■ 02 675 4200–1 ■ Open 11am–11pm daily ■ www.baan-khanitha.com ■ BB

One of the city's oldest upscale eateries serves classic Thai dishes.

Upmarket restaurant Baan Khanitha

⑦ Indus

MAP T6 ■ 71 Sukhumvit Soi 26 ■ 02 258 4900 ■ Open 11:30am–2:30pm & 6–10:30pm daily ■ BB

Indus serves contemporary Indian vegetarian and meat dishes.

⑧ Celadon

MAP Q5 ■ Sukhothai Hotel, 13/3 South Sathorn Road ■ 02 344 8888 ■ Open noon–2pm & 6–10pm daily ■ BBB

This award-winning restaurant serves sublime Thai food. The lotus pond completes the scene.

⑨ Supatra River House

MAP A4 ■ 266 Soi Wat Rakhang ■ 02 411 0305 ■ Open 11:30am–2:30pm & 5:30–10pm daily ■ BB

Excellent seafood and great riverside views at this restaurant.

⑩ Basil

MAP T6 ■ Sheraton Grande Sukhumvit, 250 Sukhumvit Road ■ 02 649 8366 ■ Open noon–2:30pm & 6–10:30pm Mon–Fri & Sun, 6–10:30pm Sat ■ BB

Diners can savor delicious Thai dishes in sophisticated surroundings.

See map on pp94–5

Bars and Pubs

1 Mikkeller Bangkok
MAP T6 ▪ 26 Yaek 2, Soi 10, Soi Ekamai, Sukhumvit Road ▪ 02 381 9891 ▪ Open 5pm–midnight daily

Located in a suburban house, this branch of the famous Danish micro-brewery offers 30 craft beers from around the world on tap.

2 Iron Balls
MAP T6 ▪ Park Lane shopping mall, Sukhumvit Soi 63 ▪ Open 6pm–1am daily

Relax amidst the wrought ironwork in a leather armchair, sipping a delicious Negroni that's made with gin from the on-site micro-distillery.

Stunning skyline views at Octave

3 Octave Rooftop Lounge Bar
MAP T6 ▪ Marriott Sukhumvit, 45th floor, Sukhumvit Soi 57 ▪ 02 797 0000 ▪ Open 5pm–2am daily

One of the best rooftop bars in the city, with 360-degree views, Octave is perfect for a sunset drink before dinner and clubbing on Soi Thonglor.

4 Nest at Le Fenix Hotel
MAP T6 ▪ 33 Sukhumvit Soi 11 ▪ 02 305 4000 ▪ Open 6pm–2am daily

Sofas and rattan beds are dotted about this bar set in stylish rooftop gardens. A retractable roof comes in handy during rainstorms.

5 Zanzibar
MAP T6 ▪ 139 Sukhumvit Soi 11 ▪ 02 651 2900 ▪ Open 9am–2am daily

Set in a lovely garden, this Italian bar and restaurant has been a hit since day one. There is a live jazz band here every night.

6 Long Table
MAP T6 ▪ 25th floor, 48 Column Tower, Sukhumvit Road, Soi 16 ▪ 02 302 2557 ▪ Open 5pm–2am daily

There are exceptional views over the city from the balconies of this achingly fashionable restaurant and bar which has an extensive food menu as well.

7 Tuba
MAP T6 ▪ 30 Soi 21, Sukhumvit Road, Soi 63 ▪ 02 711 5500 ▪ Open 11am–2am daily

A second-hand furniture shop and restaurant by day; by night a place to play pool and listen to some 70s tunes.

8 Black Swan
MAP T6 ▪ Sukhumvit Soi 19 ▪ 02 253 5141 ▪ Open 8am–1am daily

As the name suggests, this is a British-style pub offering a range of imported beers and generous portions of typical pub food.

9 Brewski
MAP T6 ▪ Radisson Blu Plaza Hotel, Sukhumvit Road ▪ 02 302 3333 ▪ Open 5pm–1am daily

This panoramic rooftop bar offers 18 craft beers and ciders on tap, plus a 100 more in bottles.

10 WTF
MAP T6 ▪ 7 Soi 51, Sukhumvit Road ▪ 02 662 6246 ▪ Open 5pm–1am Tue–Sun

A cool, Spanish-influenced bar that doubles as an art gallery, WTF offers great tapas, cocktails, and wines.

Nightclubs and Entertainment

Elaborate dance performance at Calypso Cabaret

1 Calypso Cabaret
MAP S6 ■ Asiatique the Riverfront, 2194 Charoen Krung 72–76 Road ■ 02 688 1415 ■ Show 7:30 & 9pm daily ■ Adm ■ www.calypsocabaret.com

Transvestites in sequins lip-synch and dance to pop songs *(see p55)*.

2 Glow
MAP T6 ■ 96/4–5 Sukhumvit Soi 23 ■ Open 9:30pm–3am Wed–Sun

International DJs play mostly house and techno here.

3 The Iron Fairies
MAP T6 ■ 402 Soi Thonglor ■ 09 9918 1600 ■ Open 6pm–2am daily

Like a cross between an Edwardian factory and a magical playground. Enjoy great burgers as you listen to live jazz. Book a table in advance.

4 Studio Lam
MAP T6 ■ Soi 51, Sukhumvit Road ■ 02 261 6661 ■ Open 6pm–2am Tue–Sun

DJs play great Thai folk and world music every night at this cozy and friendly neighborhood bar.

5 Tawandang German Brewery
MAP T6 ■ 462/61 Narathiwat Ratchanakharin ■ 02 678 1114–5 ■ Open 5pm–1am daily

Get a big helping of home-brewed beer while big bands play *morlam* music from northeast Thailand.

6 Lumphini Boxing Stadium
MAP T4 ■ 6 Ram Intra Road near Don Muang Airport ■ 06 2639 5596 ■ Bouts: 7pm Tue & Fri, 4 & 8:10pm Sat ■ Adm ■ www.lumpineemuaythai.com

Bangkok's second major Thai boxing stadium *(see p55)*.

7 Titanium Bar
MAP T6 ■ Sukhumvit Soi 22 ■ 02 258 3758 ■ Open 8pm–2am Mon–Sat (until 1am Sun)

Titanium boasts an ice bar and hosts "the best all-girl rock band in Thailand."

8 Living Room
MAP T6 ■ Sheraton Grande Sukhumvit, 250 Sukhumvit Road ■ 02 649 8888 ■ Open 9am–midnight daily

A stylish hang-out, Living Room features top jazz musicians every evening and at Sunday lunch.

9 Fat Gutz Saloon
MAP U5 ■ Central Eastville, Chalong Rat Expressway ■ 06 3901 1115 ■ Open 10:30am–1am daily

This place has a chic, upmarket clientele, who come for the fish and chips, and live blues performances.

10 Siam Niramit
MAP T5 ■ Ratchada Theater, 19 Tiam Ruammit Road ■ 02 649 9222 ■ Show 8pm daily ■ Adm ■ www.siamniramit.com

Experience one of the largest stage productions in the world *(see p54)*.

See map on pp94–5

TOP 10 Beyond Bangkok

Bangkok's sights are liable to cause sensory overload, from the dazzling temples to the constant crowds. Fortunately, when visitors feel they need a break, there are plenty of opportunities for a day trip or an overnight stay away from the city. Tour operators can arrange undemanding and entertaining trips to nearby attractions, such as the Floating Market and the Ancient City. For an excursion with more cultural content, head for the ruins of Ayutthaya, the country's ancient capital, or Kanchanaburi, where the bridge over the Kwai River and the Allied cemeteries mark a tragic phase of World War II. If it is tropical beaches you long for, make for Pattaya, or Koh Samed with its powder-soft sands.

A monkey at Khao Yai

BEYOND BANGKOK

① Top 10 Sights
see pp102–05

0 kilometers 40
0 miles 40

Talung
U-Thong
Bo Phloi
Suphan Buri
Ang Thong
Lopburi
Sara Buri
Muaklek
Pak Chong
Ayutthaya ⑧
Nong Khae
Khao Yai ⑤
Song Phi Nong
Bang Pa-In ②
Nong Noi
Nakhon Nayok
Prachin Buri
⑩ Kanchanaburi
Bang Len
Khok Pip
Ban Pong
Nakhon Pathom
Bangkok
Ratchasan
Chachoengsao
Damnoen Saduak Floating Market
Ratchaburi ③
Amphawa
Samut Sakhon
Suvarnabhumi
Sanam Chai Kheti
Samut Songkhram
Muang Boran (Ancient City) ④
Phana Nikhom
Khao Yoi
Pak Tho
Bight of Bangkok
Chonburi
Nong ya Pong
Phetchaburi
Ko Si Chang ①
Nong Yai
Kaeng Krachan National Park
Ban Lat
Khao Loi
Pattaya ⑨
Pluak Daeng
Koh Phal
Koh Ian
Cha Am
Koh Man Wichal
Koh Kram Yai
Bang Chang
Ban Khai
Rayong
Yang Chum
Hua Hin ⑦
Sattahip
Koh Samed ⑥
Koh Chaung

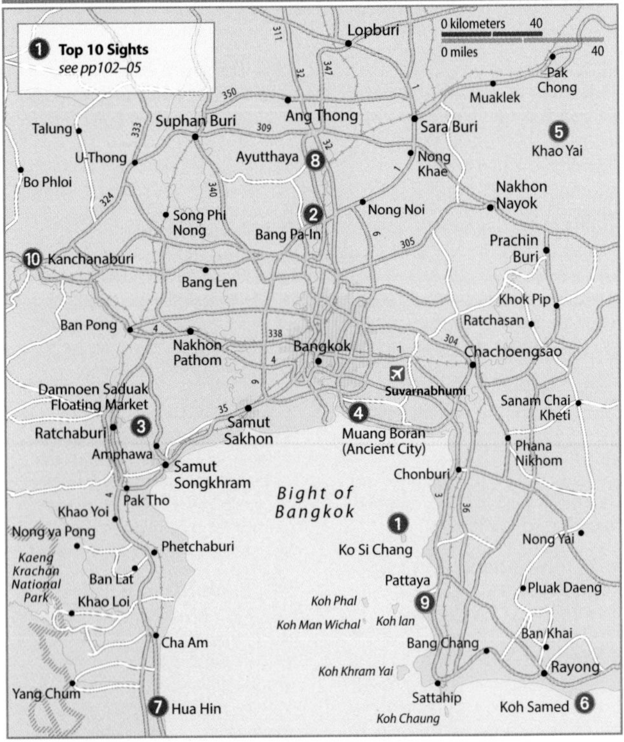

1 Koh Si Chang
MAP U3 ▪ 62 miles (99 km) SE of Bangkok

Rarely visited by foreigners, this small, rocky island is located 5 miles (8 km) off the east Gulf coast. It has a selection of every-thing – secluded beaches with clear waters, a hilly interior ripe for exploring, and the remains of Rama V's palace, plus some reasonable accommodations. The most popular beach on the island is Tham Phang Beach.

2 Bang Pa-In
While visiting Ayutthaya, it is well worth stopping off at the nearby royal retreat of Bang Pa-In. Established by King Prasat Thong (r.1629–56) in the mid-17th century and rebuilt by Rama IV and Rama V *(see p38)*, its exuber-ant buildings are an eclectic mix of Thai architecture, particularly in the Aisawan Thipphaya-at *(see p34)* pavilion, and European influences, as seen in the Phra Thinang Warophat Phiman. The manicured lawns and tranquil lakes give the place a relaxed feel.

3 Damnoen Saduak Floating Market
Although this floating market *(see pp24–5)* is considered by some to be nothing more than a show put on for tourists, it is certainly the best example of its kind. The market gives an idea of how life in this region once revolved around small boats plying their trade on narrow canals. Arrive early (or even better, stay overnight) to avoid the crowds emerging from tour buses at around 10am, and you will be rewarded with images of smiling Thais in traditional clothes, *sampans* (flat-bottomed boats) piled high with appetizing fruits, and bowls of noodles served directly from floating kitchens.

Damnoen Saduak Floating Market

4 Muang Boran (Ancient City)
MAP T2 ▪ 20 miles (33 km) from Bangkok on Sukhumvit Road, Bangpoo ▪ 02 709 1644 ▪ Open 9am–7pm daily ▪ Adm ▪ www.ancientsiam.com

Covering a huge area designed in the shape of Thailand, this cul-tural park contains reconstructions of some of the country's most famous temples and monuments. It may sound like a tacky theme park, but the site offers a visually impressive and informative expe-rience. Visitors can explore the site by car, tram, or bicycle, and it is rarely crowded.

Lakeside pavilion at Muang Boran (Ancient City)

5 Khao Yai
MAP U1 ■ 105 miles (170 km) NE of Bangkok

Thailand's first National Park, this mountainous, forested area is home to elephants, tigers, and gibbons, plus over 300 species of birds. There are several waterfalls and bat caves, as well as resorts and golf courses in the foothills outside the park's boundaries. Trekking and mountain biking tours are offered, as well as camping. Visitors should plan on spending the night here to fully appreciate this natural wonderland.

6 Koh Samed
MAP U3 ■ 124 miles (200 km) SE of Bangkok

Easily the best beach escape from the capital, Koh Samed is an island with clear waters and fine sand, as well as a national park. Due to its popularity, accommodation rates have spiraled. By avoiding weekends and public holidays, it is possible to enjoy the idyllic surroundings without feeling like a sardine in a can.

Crystal-clear waters of Koh Samed

7 Hua Hin
MAP S3 ■ 118 miles (190 km) SW of Bangkok

Thailand's oldest beach resort was popularized by the royal family when they had a summer palace built here in 1926. Though the 3-mile (5-km) beach is fine for a stroll or a pony ride, shade is limited, and the shallow bay can frustrate swimmers. Vestiges of the past remain in the train station and the squid piers along the front.

Ancient ruins at Ayutthaya

8 Ayutthaya
From 1350 to 1767, Ayutthaya ruled supreme as the capital of its own kingdom, only to be abandoned after being sacked by the Burmese (see p38). The Ayutthaya Historical Park features ancient ruins set in tranquil countryside. The main temples – Wat Ratchaburana, Wat Mahathat, and Wat Sri Sanphet (see pp32–5) – can be covered in a day trip.

9 Pattaya
MAP U3 ■ 91 miles (147 km) SE of Bangkok

Pattaya is infamous for its go-go bars, discos, transvestite cabarets, and countless "bar beers" – open-sided bars with friendly hostesses. Yet the town has made an attempt to clean up its image, and there are now some family attractions, such as Pattaya Park Water Park, Mini Siam, Underwater World, and an Elephant Village. Watersports and golf are

---

THE DEATH RAILWAY

Between 1942–3, about 16,000 Allied prisoners of war and 90,000 Asians died during the construction of a railroad line from Thailand to Burma. The Japanese saw the line as crucial to their occupation of Southeast Asia. After the Japanese surrender, the British tore up the track. The rail link was never re-established.

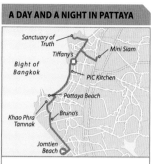

Sanctuary of Truth

Tiffany's

Mini Siam

Bight of Bangkok

PIC Kitchen

Pattaya Beach

Khao Phra Tamnak

Bruno's

Jomtien Beach

▶ MORNING

Start the day relaxing on Jomtien Beach, on the endless stretch of sand just south of **Pattaya** town center. Take a swim to cool down or if you are feeling energetic have go waterskiing, windsurfing, or parasailing. If you haven't been snacking all morning on seafood or fruit sold by wandering vendors on the beach, head for **Bruno's** *(Map U3; Tabphaya Road; 03 811 9586; open noon–2:30pm & 6pm–late daily)* near the north end of the beach for a steak or lobster lunch.

AFTERNOON

After lunch, head up to Khao Phra Tamnak from where there are excellent views of Pattaya Beach. Next, head north of town to the Sanctuary of Truth, a fabulous palace that blends influences from Khmer, Hindu, and Buddhist architecture. Finish the afternoon's sightseeing with a visit to **Mini Siam**, which features miniature models of some of the country's most famous buildings.

NIGHT

Begin your evening in any of the beachfront beer bars, to get a feel for the party mood of the town. For dinner, go to **PIC Kitchen** *(Map U3; Soi 5; 03 842 8374; open 11am–2pm & 5pm–midnight daily)* and indulge in a delicious curry. Next, check out a Thai transvestite cabaret at Tiffany's. After the show, either head for bed or explore Pattaya's pulsating nightlife.

also big here, and there are some excellent seafood restaurants and well-stocked shopping malls.

⑩ Kanchanaburi
MAP S2 ▪ 80 miles (130 km) W of Bangkok

At the western edge of the Central Plains, Kanchanaburi is a popular day trip from Bangkok. The main sights are the bridge over the Kwai River and the war cemeteries where thousands of allied soldiers who died in World War II during the construction of the "Death Railway" to Burma are buried. The Thailand-Burma Railway Center explains how the disastrous events unfolded. Kanchanaburi is also the jumping-off point for several natural sites, including the Erawan National Park, with its waterfalls.

Waterfalls near Kanchanaburi

See map on p102 ←

Streetsmart

Preparing and selling boat noodles
at a floating market in Bangkok

Getting To and Around
  Bangkok   **108**

Practical Information   **110**

Places to Stay   **114**

General Index   **118**

Acknowledgments   **124**

Phrase Book   **126**

Getting To and Around Bangkok

Arriving by Air

Most travelers to Bangkok arrive by air, unless entering Thailand via a land crossing from Malaysia, Cambodia, Laos, or Myanmar. The city's airport **Suvarnabhumi International Airport (BKK)** hosts over 80 airlines with direct flights from most major cities. There is one terminal operating, international and domestic flights, with arrivals on Level 2 and departures on Level 4. The airport is around 16 miles (25 km) east of Bangkok.

16 miles (25 km) north of Bangkok is the old international airport, **Don Muang International Airport (DMK).** It operates domestic and international low-cost airlines such as Nok Air, Air Asia, and Thai Lion Air. Thai Airways has an extensive network, and budget airlines that operate flights within Thailand and to destinations in Southeast Asia and beyond.

The Suvarnabhumi Airport Rail Link (SARL) leaves from the basement of the airport terminal and transfers into the city for minimal costs. It also connects with Bangkok's two MRT (mass rapid transit) systems – the Skytrain and the subway.

Metered taxis from both airports charge a B50 pick-up fee. There are tolls to pay on the overhead expressways as well.

Arriving by Train

It is possible to reach Bangkok from Singapore and Malaysia by train.

Most trains terminate at **Hua Lampong Station.** Trains from Kanchanaburi, and some from Hua Hin, terminate at **Thonburi Station.**

Arriving by Bus

Thailand offers overland itineraries that include visits to neighboring countries. Buses from Malaysia terminate at the **Southern Bus Terminal,** while those from Cambodia and Laos arrive at the **Northern Bus Terminal** at Mochit.

Traveling by Skytrain

Bangkok's first and most useful mass rapid transit system, the **Skytrain (BTS)**. It is an elevated railway with two lines. The Sukhumvit Line runs from Chatuchak Weekend Market, through the downtown area at Rama I and Ploenchit roads, along Sukhumvit Road to Soi Thonglor, and into the eastern suburbs. The Silom Line runs from the National Stadium (near Jim Thompson House), through the downtown Silom area, to Saphan Taksin (good for accessing river boats), and over the river into Thonburi. The two lines intersect at Siam Square. The Skytrain links to the high-speed SARL at Phaya Thai Station.

It gets busy during rush hours (7–9am and 5–7pm). To avoid lines at the ticket vending machines, go to the manned ticket counters and buy a one-day pass for B140 (unlimited trips) or a Rabbit Card (stored-value card) for

B200. The last train is at midnight.

Traveling by MRT

The **MRT** system's main Blue Line covers a 12-mile (20-km) underground loop from Hua Lampong Station, passing through Silom and Sukhumvit downtown areas, and continuing to Chatuchak Weekend Market. Extension work is underway, and the route will continue from Hua Lampong into Chinatown, the Old City, and western suburbs.

The MRT intersects with the Skytrain at three stations. Transferring between them requires buying a new ticket. It connects with the SARL at Makkasan Station.

The MRT offers day passes and stored-value cards. Like the Skytrain, it gets busy during rush hours, and it's best to plan trips outside those times if possible. The last train is at midnight.

Traveling by Boat

Chao Phraya and **Khlong Saen Saeb** express boat services *(see p21)* are good for sightseeing and transportation, especially to go from Downtown to the Old City until the new MRT stations open. Hotels on the Thonburi side offer free shuttles. Chartering a longtail boat is an option.

Traveling by Bus

BMTA runs an extensive bus network with very cheap fares. Most routes operate 4am–10pm, with a few providing a 24-hour service. Buses can get stuck in heavy traffic, so an air-conditioned bus is a good option.

Traveling by Car

Without detailed road knowledge, city driving can be very frustrating. Car rental companies such as **Hertz** and **Budget** also offer drivers.

Traveling by Taxi

Metered taxis are easy to find and relatively cheap, with a flag fare of B35 for the first 0.6 miles (1 km) and B5.5 for every 0.6 mile (1 km) after that (though an increase of 5 per cent has recently been proposed). The meter also calculates time, charging for slow-moving traffic. A short journey costs about B60. Insist on using the meter, since it is cheaper

than negotiating a fare. App-based taxi services such as **All Thai Taxi** (uses standard Thai taxis) and **Grab** (choice of vehicle) operate in Bangkok.

Traveling by Motorbike Taxi

Motorbike taxi riders wait on the corners of important roads. They are useful for routes that cannot be covered by other modes of transport. Fares are negotiable, starting at B20 for a short trip. They are fast and can squeeze through traffic jams, but can be dangerous, so hang tight.

Traveling by Bicycle

Bike-shares and rentals exist here, and the Old City has dedicated bike lanes, but it's best to start with a cycling tour. Try **Follow Me**, **Pun Pun Bike Share**, or **Spice Roads**.

Traveling by Tuk-Tuk

A ride in a tuk-tuk is an essential part of the Thai experience, and it can be exciting weaving through traffic in these open-sided three-wheelers. However, they are noisy and unprotected from pollution. Fares must be negotiated before you start.

Traveling on Foot

The key to a pleasant walk in Bangkok is to avoid major thoroughfares and walk in the quiet *sois* (lanes) that run parallel to the main roads. Use a good street map to plot your route via the *sois*. Dedicated walkers should try to find a copy of Ken Barrett's excellent *22 Walks in Bangkok*, or join a guided walking tour.

DIRECTORY

ARRIVING BY AIR

Don Muang International Airport (DMK)
w donmuangairport.com

Suvarnabhumi International Airport (BKK)
w suvarnabhumi airport.com

ARRIVING BY TRAIN

Hua Lampong Station
MAP F6 ▪ Rama IV Rd
02 225 6964

Thonburi Station
MAP A3 ▪ Siriraj, Bangkok Noi

ARRIVING BY BUS

Northern Bus Terminal
MAP T5 ▪
Phahonyothin Rd
02 272 0299

Southern Bus Terminal
MAP S5 ▪ Borommarat Chonnani Rd
02 435 1199

TRAVELING BY SKYTRAIN

Skytrain (BTS)
w bts.co.th

TRAVELING BY MRT

MRT
w bemplc.co.th

TRAVELING BY BOAT

Chao Phraya
w chaophrayaexpress boat.com

Khlong Saen Saeb
w khlongsaensaep.com

TRAVELING BY BUS

BMTA
w bmta.co.th

TRAVELING BY CAR

Budget
w budget.co.th

TRAVELING BY TAXI

All Thai Taxi
w allthaitaxi.com

Grab
w grab.com

Hertz
w hertzthailand.com

TRAVELING BY BICYCLE

Follow Me
w followmebiketour. com

Pun Pun Bike Share
w punpunbikeshare. com

Spice Roads
w spiceroads.com

Practical Information

Passports and Visas

Visitors to Thailand must have a passport valid for at least six months from the date of entry. People from most Western countries are given a 30-day tourist visa on-arrival at the airport. For longer visits, apply at the nearest Thai embassy for a 60-day visa, which must be used within three months of issue. Non-immigrant 90-day visas are available if there is a good reason for extending a stay, such as education or business. Visas for 30 or 60 days can be extended by 30 days at the **Immigration Office** for a fee. If you overstay your visa, there is a B500 fine per day. These regulations are subject to change, so check the **Thai Ministry of Foreign Affairs** website.

Numerous countries, including **Australia**, the **UK**, and the **US**, have consular representation in the city.

Customs and Immigration

Duty-free allowance for visitors arriving in Thailand is 200 cigarettes or 9 oz (250 g) of tobacco or a liter of wines or spirits. E-cigarettes and pornography are banned. Checks of incoming tourists is cursory at best.

Travel Safety Advice

Visitors can get up-to-date travel safety information from the **UK Foreign and Commonwealth Office**, the **US Department of State**, and the **Australian Department of Foreign Affairs and Trade**.

Travel Insurance

Travel insurance is strongly recommended, as health-care can be costly. Be sure to double check that your policy covers Thailand, along with theft and accidental loss, before traveling.

Health

Healthcare is affordable, and the country is popular for medical tourism. **Bangkok Nursing Home (BNH) Hospital** and **Bumrungrad Hospital** are good for serious issues and surgery. In an emergency, call the **Medical Hotline**. For minor ailments, local clinics are hygienic and reliable, and staff speak some English. Pharmacies are usually well stocked. Prescriptions are not required for antibiotics. Dental care at places such as the **Dental Hospital** is inexpensive and good. Contact your healthcare provider at home for recommended pre-travel vaccinations. Malaria is not a significant threat in Bangkok, but sexually transmitted diseases are a problem so protection is suggested.

Personal Security

Bangkok is fairly safe, but it is wise to store cash in your hotel safe. Avoid wearing expensive jewelry in public and watch out for pickpockets in crowded areas and ensure bags are theft-proof. Violent incidents are rare and usually linked to too much alcohol, as are assaults on women. Avoid political demonstrations here.

Emergency Services

In case of emergency contact the **Tourist Police**, which has an English-speaking operator. Lines are open from 8am to midnight. The **Metropolitan Mobile Police** covers general emergencies.

Travelers with Specific Needs

Thailand has improved wheelchair accessibility, in many hotels and departmental stores by providing ramps and elevators. Sidewalks are not wheelchair-friendly. However, what the city lacks in infrastructure for the disabled, is made up by the helpful nature of the people. Specialized tour agencies cater to those with specific needs. **Help and Care** offers accessible holidays and other services.

Currency and Banking

Thailand's currency is the *baht* (B), divided into 100 *satang*. There are B1, B2, B5, and B10 coins; notes are available for B20 (green), B50 (blue), B100 (red), B500 (purple), and B1,000 (brown).

Most banks, including **Bangkok Bank** and **Thai Military Bank**, are open 8:30am–3:30pm Monday–Friday, but branches in airports and department stores often stay open later and on weekends. Big branches have a foreign-exchange counter, can arrange international transfers, and offer the best exchange rate.

ATMs can be found outside bank branches, mini-marts, and department stores. All offer an English-language option and accept major credit and debit cards, but a service charge is applied.

VISA and MasterCard credit and debit cards are accepted by major banks, travel agents, department stores, hotels, and most restaurants. American Express and Diners Club are not widely accepted.

Postal Services

Post office hours are normally 8:30am–4:30pm Monday–Friday and 9am–noon on Saturday. Letters to or from Europe or the US take at least a week to arrive. For important documents, use the Express Mail Service (EMS) or pay a fee to register the letter.

Television, Radio, and Newspapers

Some guesthouses and many hotels offer cable TV with English channels. There are also a few radio stations that broadcast in English, such as **Eazy FM** and **Radio Thailand**. Two English dailies, **Bangkok Post** and **The Nation**, carry news and listings. Copies of international papers such as the UK's *The Times* and *USA Today* are sold in some bookshops, though prices for these are steep.

Opening Hours

Most government offices are open 8:30am–4:30pm on weekdays, but many close for lunch. Tourist attractions tend to open 9am–5pm daily.

Department stores open daily at 10am and close at 9 or 10pm. On public holidays, government offices, post offices, and banks are closed, but most shops, bars and restaurants remain open.

Time Difference

Thailand is 7 hours ahead of Greenwich Mean Time, 12 hours ahead of US Eastern Standard Time, and three hours behind Australian Eastern Standard Time.

Electrical Appliances

The electrical current in Thailand flows at 220 volts AC, 50 Hz, and most plug sockets are of the two-pin variety. Adaptors are readily available in department stores.

DIRECTORY

PASSPORTS AND VISAS

Australia
w thailand.embassy.gov.au

Immigration Office
w bangkok.immigration.go.th

Thai Ministry of Foreign Affairs
w mfa.go.th

UK
w gov.uk/government/world/organisations/british-embassy-bangkok

US
w th.usembassy.gov

TRAVEL SAFETY ADVICE

Australian Department of Foreign Affairs and Trade
w dfat.gov.au
w smartraveller.gov.au

UK Foreign and Commonwealth Office
w gov.uk/foreign-travel-advice

US Department of State
w travel.state.gov

HEALTH

BNH Hospital
w bnhhospital.com

Bumrungrad Hospital
w bumrungrad.com

Dental Hospital
w dentalhospitalbangkok.com

Medical Hotline
c 1669

EMERGENCY SERVICES

Metropolitan Mobile Police
c 191

Tourist Police
c 1155
w touristpolice.go.th

TRAVELERS WITH SPECIFIC NEEDS

Help and Care
w wheelchairtours.com

CURRENCY AND BANKING

Bangkok Bank
c 1333, +662 645 5555 (from abroad)
w bangkokbank.com

Thai Military Bank
c 1558, +662 299 1558 (from abroad)
w tmbbank.com

TELEVISION, RADIO, AND NEWSPAPERS

Bangkok Post
w bangkokpost.com

Eazy FM
w eazyfm.becteroradio.com

Radio Thailand
w hsk9.org

The Nation
w nationmultimedia.com

Weather

The best time to visit is November–February, with clear skies and cooler temperatures, generally around 80° F (26.5° C). However, hotel rates tend to be higher, and tourist attractions more crowded. The hot season (March–May) is fine for a beach holiday but not for sight-seeing. The rainy season (June–October) can be pleasant, and storms usually blow over quickly.

The tropical monsoon climate means that spring is hot, followed by sum-mer rains. Loose, breath-able clothes are best, and layering a long-sleeved top over a T-shirt also provides sun protection. Bangkokians see short pants as beachwear, but visitors are given latitude, except in temples. During the rainy season umbrella vendors are everywhere.

Visitor Information

The **Tourism Authority of Thailand**, the official gov-ernment tourist board, has offices worldwide and its headquarters in Bangkok. Its website provides com-prehensive coverage of destinations and events, and maps and brochures are available from its office. The **Bangkok Tourism Division** is also a useful source of information and has booths in many of the city's tourist areas.

Some of the best travel tips come from two monthly magazines, *Bangkok 101* and *The Big Chilli*, which are sold in bookstores (although both have good websites). Mainly directed toward expats, they offer the latest in dining,

nightlife, and exploring, and are much more reliable than the many blogs and click-driven websites. *BK's* website and magazine, distributed free in hotels, also offers useful listings.

Trips and Tours

Planning a journey in a crowded, unfamiliar city can be difficult, so many people opt for a guided tour. While such tours may be enjoyable and informative, they are also expensive and preclude encounters with local people that can lead to stimulating cultural exchanges. We recom-mend self-guiding for the major sites (*see Exploring Bangkok, pp6–7*) and using tours focused on special interests, such as culinary tours, tours organized by art museums, or activities requiring special equip-ment, such as cycling.

Shopping

Bangkok is a shopper's paradise and runs the gamut from the glitziest malls to sidewalk ven-dors. The massive and ultra-modern shopping malls in Siam Square and Sukhumvit are like small cities, containing department stores, food courts, bowling alleys, designer boutiques, and skating rinks. Shopping in markets and at street stalls combines the opportunity to pick up bargains with cultural interaction. The best markets for textiles or ready-made clothes are Chatuchak (*see pp26–7*), Phahurat (*see p77*), and Pratunam (*see p60*), while street stalls in

Khao San Road, Patpong, and Sukhumvit Road are good for souvenirs.

Prices are fixed in shopping malls and boutiques, but bargaining is expected in markets and at street stalls, where vendors quote a price that may be up to double the object's value. Start by offering a figure less than what you are prepared to pay and gradually increase the offer until a deal is struck. Keep smiling! If all else fails, walking away may persuade a vendor to drop the price.

Thai handicrafts make great souvenirs and gifts. These are widely available in Bangkok at markets such as Chatuchak. Items on offer include clothes as well as silk and cotton bags, lacquerware, wall hangings, ceramics, bas-kets and woodcarvings. Gold in Thailand is 24 karat and sold by weight, its value varying according to the world market. Colored gems such as rubies and sapphires are very alluring, but unless you are an expert, confine any purchases to high-end shops, such as those in **Peninsula Plaza**, since inferior gems and fakes abound. Custom-tailored clothing is also of interest, but only the best shops, like **Tailor on Ten**, use fabrics of high quality, and several fittings are required for a good result. Antiques are also worth considering, but similar to newly cast Buddha images, they require a special export permit from the Department of Fine Arts. The export of antique Buddhas is forbidden.

Thais produce excellent copies of anything from

branded watches to designer clothes. Western countries' customs take fakes seriously, and confiscation – or even prosecution – is possible.

Dining

While in Bangkok, you can eat in fancy restaurants, at street stalls, and everywhere in between. While only a few restaurants are expensive, some of Bangkok's best food can be found at street stalls, so be adventurous and try everything. Choose street food in places off the main roads, where it's cooler and quieter. Don't miss the food courts found in most shopping malls – the prices are only slightly above street-food prices, and the air-conditioning makes things more comfortable. Food courts use a coupon system – you pay at a central kiosk rather than paying the vendors.

Thais love children, and even if kids' menus are rare, taking children along for a meal makes everyone happy.

The concept of tipping, once alien to Thais, has been happily embraced by restaurant staff. This is especially true for tourist areas. The 10–15 percent rule followed in the West does not apply in Bangkok. Leave whatever you think the staff deserve; every *baht* will be appreciated. High-end restaurants often add a service charge; if so, no tip is necessary.

Accommodation

In Bangkok, five-star accommodation can cost as little as a mid-range hotel in Europe or the US. For your money, you can expect a large room with a decent view, luxurious furnishings and decor, plenty of on-site bars and restaurants and attentive service *(see pp114–15).*

Mid-range hotels offer all the basic comforts, like air-conditioned rooms, bathrooms with hot water, and television, though without the luxurious touches and elegance of top-end hotels. It is also well worth checking out the rapidly growing number of boutique hotels that offer a more personal touch and unique character, often missing even in top-end hotels *(see pp115–16).*

Bangkok attracts a stream of budget tourists, mostly to Khao San Road, the "backpackers' ghetto." A typical cheap room will be small, often without windows, with a bed, a fan, paperthin walls, and shared bathrooms. Khao San Road is great for dining and nightlife, but nearby areas are worth exploring for quieter accommodations *(see p117).* **Agoda** is a useful booking resource. **Airbnb**, the online peer-to-peer accommodation service, also operates in Bangkok and offers good opportunities to meet with and get to know locals.

It is a good idea to book your hotel room well in advance of your visit, especially if the hotel in question is highly rated, and even more so during the high season (Nov–Feb) or major festivals. Internet booking services are useful, but be sure to check change and cancellation policies before booking. Some hotels offer good rates on their own websites. If using Airbnb, doublecheck the location of the property, since many of the listings are far from the center of the city.

Hotel rates hit a peak during the cool season (Nov–Feb), when many establishments operate at full occupancy. For the rest of the year, it is worth asking about discounts, especially if you plan to stay several nights. Some budget hotels and guesthouses also offer competitive monthly rates.

DIRECTORY

VISITOR INFORMATION

Bangkok Tourism Division
MAP C2 ▪ 17/1 Phra Athit Road
☎ 02 225 7612–4
ⓦ facebook.com/ tourismdivision

Tourism Authority of Thailand
Off MAP R2 ▪ 1600 Petchaburi Road
☎ 1672 (toll-free)
ⓦ tourismthailand.org

SHOPPING

Peninsula Plaza
MAP Q3 ▪ 153 Ratchadamri Road
☎ 02 253 9791

Tailor on Ten
MAP T6
▪ Sukhumvit Soi 8
☎ (084) 877 1543

ACCOMMODATION

Agoda
ⓦ agoda.com

Airbnb
ⓦ airbnb.com

Places to Stay

PRICE CATEGORIES
For a standard, double room per night (with breakfast if included), taxes and extra charges.

B under B1,800　　**BB** B1,800–4,000　　**BBB** over B4,000

Luxury Hotels

Anantara Bangkok Riverside Resort and Spa
MAP S6 ▪ 257 Charoen Nakhon Road, Thonburi ▪ 02 476 0022 ▪ www.anantara.com ▪ BBB
Built on prime property on the west bank of the Chao Phraya River, this huge complex has a lovely spa, fine gardens, many restaurants, and an exotic pool. Each room has a private balcony.

Anantara Siam
MAP Q3 ▪ 55 Ratchadamri Road ▪ 02 126 8866 ▪ www.anantara.com ▪ BBB
Luxurious rooms, impeccable service, and a number of fine-dining restaurants make this one of Bangkok's best hotels. It is in an excellent location, with views over the green expanse of the Royal Bangkok Sports Club.

COMO Metropolitan Bangkok
MAP Q5 ▪ 27 South Sathorn Road ▪ 02 625 3333 ▪ www.comohotels.com ▪ BBB
Bangkok's trendiest hotel features a minimalist look and silk furnishings. Its two great restaurants, Nahm and Glow (see p101), and the members-only Met Bar attract the city's top design gurus.

Conrad Hotel
MAP R3 ▪ All Seasons Place, Withayu Road ▪ 02 690 9999 ▪ www.conradhotels.com ▪ BBB
Designed in contemporary Thai style, making lavish use of silk and wood, Conrad Hotel has lovely views over Lumphini Park (see p86). It has a central location, and its restaurants and bars are among the best in town.

Grand Hyatt Erawan Bangkok
MAP Q3 ▪ 494 Ratchadamri Road ▪ 02 254 1234 ▪ www.hyatt.com ▪ BBB
A grandiose entrance leads to guest rooms with large windows, marble baths, and trendy fittings. The afternoon tea in the Garden Lounge is a delight.

Mandarin Oriental Hotel
MAP M5 ▪ 48 Oriental Avenue ▪ 02 659 9000 ▪ www.mandarinoriental.com/bangkok ▪ BBB
The historic Oriental (see p85) has often been voted the world's best hotel for its superb facilities, exceptional views, and personalized service.

The Peninsula Hotel
MAP L5 ▪ 333 Charoen Nakhon Road ▪ 02 020 2888 ▪ www.bangkok.peninsula.com ▪ BBB
The Peninsula has won several awards for its wave-shaped design and spacious guest rooms with fabulous views of the Chao Phraya River and the city. It has a three-tiered swimming pool, a gorgeous spa and restaurants serving Thai, and Cantonese cuisine.

Royal Orchid Sheraton
MAP M4 ▪ 2 Captain Bush Lane ▪ 02 266 0123 ▪ www.marriott.com ▪ BBB
This 28-story hotel has pools and tennis courts, a fitness center and spa, restaurants serving royal Thai and Italian cuisine, and a relaxed riverside bar.

Shangri-La Hotel
MAP M6 ▪ 89 Soi Wat Suan Phlu, Charoen Krung Road ▪ 02 236 7777 ▪ www.shangri-la.com ▪ BBB
With 800 rooms, the riverside Shangri-La is one of Bangkok's biggest luxury hotels. It has several restaurants and bars; the excellent Chi, The Spa (see p44); a fitness center, pools, and tennis courts.

Siam Kempinski Hotel
MAP P2 ▪ 991/9 Rama I Road ▪ 02 162 9000 ▪ www.kempinski.com/bangkok ▪ BBB
An Art Deco-inspired resort hotel in the heart of the city, the beautiful Siam Kempinski is set around a landscaped garden and has three pools. It also has a spa and an excellent contemporary Thai restaurant.

Sukhothai Hotel

MAP Q5 ■ 13/3 South Sathorn Road ■ 02 344 8888 ■ www.sukhothai. com ■ BBB

This hotel blends modern conveniences and traditional Thai architecture. Surrounded by lush gardens and pools, the hotel has luxurious rooms, three excellent restaurants, and a pool-terrace café.

W Hotel

MAP P6 ■ 106 North Sathorn Road ■ 02 344 4000 ■ www.marriott. com ■ BBB

Chic and sleek, this oasis of modern luxury also includes The House on Sathorn, a colonial mansion that once housed the Russian Embassy, now a sumptuous restaurant and bar. Their Woo Bar is a Bangkok hot spot.

Business Hotels

Majestic Grande Sukhumvit

MAP T6 ■ 12 Sukhumvit Soi 2 ■ 02 262 2999 ■ www.majesticgrande. com ■ BB

Conveniently located, this opulent hotel offers an excellent range of facilities for business guests, including generous desk space in the rooms and a translation service in the business center.

InterContinental Hotel

MAP R3 ■ 973 Ploenchit Road ■ 02 656 0444 ■ www.intercontinental. com ■ BBB

Towering above Ploenchit's business district, this 37-story hotel is perfect for business travelers and shoppers, with the Skytrain

right at its doorstep. Huge rooms offer great views from the double-glazed, soundproofed windows.

Lebua at State Tower

MAP N5 ■ 1055 Silom Road ■ 02 624 9999 ■ www.lebua.com ■ BBB

This distinctive skyscraper with its golden dome is one of Bangkok's icons. It is also home to Breeze (see p91) and Sirocco, two of the city's top dining venues, as well as the stunning Sky Bar (see p92).

Marriott Marquis Queens Park

MAP T6 ■ 199 Sukhumvit Soi 22 ■ 02 059 5555 ■ www.marriott.com ■ BBB

The luxurious rooms at this hotel overlook Benjasiri Park. It boasts two swimming pools and also houses a spa. There's a plethora of eateries including a Thai–Western tea room, as well as a contemporary Asian restaurant on the rooftop.

Sheraton Grande Sukhumvit

MAP T6 ■ 250 Sukhumvit Road ■ 02 649 8888 ■ www.sheratongrande-sukhumvit.com ■ BBB

Among Bangkok's best business hotels, the Sheraton Grande offers modern elegance with state-of-the-art facilities. Its business center is open 24 hours, and a footbridge connects the hotel to the Asoke Skytrain station.

Westin Grande Sukhumvit

MAP T6 ■ 259 Sukhumvit Road ■ 02 207 8000 ■ www.marriott.com ■ BBB

The rooms are designed with executive travelers in

mind, complete with soft beds and writing desks. The Vareena Spa and the Zest Bar and Terrace have panoramic views.

Mid-Range Hotels

Aloft Hotel Bangkok

MAP T6 ■ 35 Sukhumvit Soi 11 ■ 02 207 7000 ■ www.aloftbangkok-sukhumvit11.com ■ BB

Sheraton's mid-range chain provides trendy decor, large rooms, and efficient service. Levels (see p93), one of the city's hottest nightspots, is on the sixth floor. Soi 11 has many cafés and pubs.

Chillax Resort

MAP C2 ■ 274 Samsen Road Soi 2 ■ 02 629 4400 ■ www.chillaxresort.com ■ BB

This high-rise hotel has a rooftop infinity pool with incredible views over the city and the river. Each room has a Jacuzzi, good for unwinding after a long day's sightseeing.

Navalai River Resort

MAP C2 ■ 45 Phra Athit Road ■ 02 280 9955 ■ www.navalai.com ■ BB

Located on hip Phra Athit Road, near the Grand Palace, the Navalai has balconied rooms overlooking the Chao Phraya and a rooftop pool. There is also a riverside restaurant.

New Siam Riverside

MAP B2 ■ 21 Phra Athit Road ■ 02 629 3535 ■ www.newsiam.net ■ BB

This clean and quiet inn offers the best value rooms on the river in the lively Phra Athit area, near Khao San Road.

Rembrandt Hotel
MAP T6 ▪ 19 Sukhumvit
Soi 18 ▪ 02 261 7100
▪ www.rembrandtbkk.
com ▪ BB
In a quiet *soi* off the main
Sukhumvit Road, near
Soi Asok, the Rembrandt
offers value well beyond
its price and immaculate
rooms, as well as the
best Indian and Mexican
restaurants in the city.

The Rose Hotel
MAP P5 ▪ 118 Surawong
Road ▪ 02 266 8268
▪ www.rosehotelbkk.
com ▪ BB
Close to much of the
Silom area's shopping
and nightlife, the Rose
offers comfortable, quiet
rooms in contemporary
Asian style. It has a
swimming pool, an
excellent restaurant,
a gym, and a sauna.

Boutique Hotels

Luxx Hotel
MAP N5 ▪ 6/11 Decho
Road ▪ 02 635 8800
▪ www.staywithluxx.
com ▪ BB
The minimalist appearance
of the suites and compact
rooms at this hotel will
appeal to the young, hip,
and trendy; and the loca-
tion, just a few steps
from the shops and
nightlife of Silom Road,
could not be better.

Shanghai Mansion
MAP L3 ▪ 479–81
Yaowarat Road ▪ 02 221
2121 ▪ www.shanghai
mansion.com ▪ BB
In the heart of Chinatown,
this chic and unusual
hotel has just over 50
smallish rooms fitted
with four-poster beds and
painted in vibrant colors.
Some are windowless.

There is a restaurant,
massage/spa facilities,
and a shuttle tuk-tuk
service for guests.

Siam Heritage
MAP P5 ▪ 115/1 Surawong
Road ▪ 02 353 6166
▪ www.thesiamheritage.
com ▪ BB
The rooms of this hotel
are decorated in Northern
and Central Thai style,
with polished wood floors
and antique-style furnishings. Services include
a spa, a bakery, and a
Thai restaurant.

AriyasomVilla Boutique Hotel
MAP T6 ▪ 65 Sukhumvit
Soi 1 ▪ 02 254 8880 ▪ www.
ariyasom.com ▪ BBB
This 1940s mansion
is a serene urban oasis
close to the Saen Saeb
canal and downtown
shopping areas. There's
a lovely garden and pool,
and great vegetarian food.

Chakrabongse Villas
MAP B5 ▪ 396 Maharaj
Road ▪ 02 222 1290
▪ www.thaivillas.com
▪ BBB
Located on the Chao
Phraya River, near Wat
Pho and with amazing
views of Wat Arun, this
stunning hotel comprises
seven rooms and suites
set in lush tropical gar-
dens, with a pool and
riverside dining terrace.

Praya Palazzo
MAP B2 ▪ 757/1 Somdet
Phra Pin Klao Road, Soi 2
▪ 02 883 2998 ▪ www.
prayapalazzo.com ▪ BBB
With a riverfront location
on the Thonburi side, this
restored Italianate mansion
is beautifully decorated
and serves excellent
Thai and Western food.

The Siam
MAP S5 ▪ 3/2 Khao Road,
behind Vachira Hospital
▪ 02 206 6999 ▪ www.
thesiamhotel.com ▪ BBB
Bangkok's top-rated
small hotel, located
in the quiet Dusit area,
has 39 sumptuously
decorated suites and
villas with antique
furniture and lovely
views of the river.

Budget

A-One Inn
MAP P2 ▪ 25/13 Soi
Kasemsan 1, Rama I
Road ▪ 02 215 3029
▪ www.aoneinn.com ▪ B
Tucked just around
the corner from Siam
Square, the shoppers'
paradise, this upscale
guesthouse has basic
but clean rooms. The
staff are friendly, there
is Wi-Fi throughout,
and it is only a few
steps from the National
Stadium BTS station.

Jim's Lodge
MAP R3 ▪ 25/7 Soi
Ruamrudee, Ploenchit
Road ▪ 02 255 3100 ▪ B
Located near several
major embassies and
shopping malls, Jim's
Lodge offers good-sized,
well-equipped standard
and superior rooms,
as well as suites. Service
is very efficient, and the
lodge's other amenities
include a restaurant.

New Siam 2
MAP B2 ▪ 50 Trok Rong
Mai, Phra Athit Road
▪ 02 282 2795 ▪ www.
newsiam.net ▪ B
This modern budget
hotel offers peace and
privacy near the Grand
Palace. Rooms are
well equipped with

in-room safes and private bathrooms, while air-conditioning costs extra. There is a small swimming pool.

Riverview Guesthouse

MAP E6 ▪ 768 Songwat Road ▪ 02 234 5429 ▪ www.riverviewbkk. com ▪ B
Located in a backstreet beside the San Jao Sien Khong temple in Chinatown, this family-run guesthouse has refurbished rooms and good views of the Chao Phraya River from the upper floors. There is a great rooftop bar and restaurant.

Silom Village Inn

MAP N5 ▪ 286 Silom Road ▪ 02 635 6810 ▪ www.silomvillage.co. th/hotel_silom.php ▪ B
Set in Bangkok's most famous nightlife district, this small hotel is housed in a shopping complex that recreates the atmosphere of a traditional Thai village. It offers standard and deluxe rooms, as well as suites at affordable rates. There are nightly cultural shows at the adjoining entertainment hall.

Wall Street Inn

MAP P5 ▪ 37/20–24 Surawong Road ▪ 02 233 4144 ▪ www.wallstreet innhotel.com ▪ B
The smartly furnished rooms in this hotel come with comfortable beds, cable TV, and minibars. There is also a business center, a coffee shop, and a massage parlor offering traditional massage and foot reflexology.

Beyond Bangkok

Away Kanchanaburi Dheva Mantra Resort & Spa

MAP S2 ▪ Moo 3, Thamakham Road, Kanchanaburi ▪ 034 615 999 ▪ www.away resorts.com ▪ BB
The sumptuous rooms here are set in an elegant colonial-style building and surrounded by huge gardens. Although it is a bit out of town, there are some great views over the river and mountains. There's also an excellent spa.

Bangkok Tree House

MAP T6 ▪ 60 Moo 1, Petch Cha Hueng Road, Bang Namphueng ▪ 08 2995 1150 ▪ www.bangkok treehouse.com ▪ BB
A boutique eco-resort located in Bang Krajao, Bangkok's green lung (see p49), the Tree House is accessible only by boat or on foot. So close yet so different from the metropolis, it offers organic food and free bicycles – ideal for exploring this rural area.

Kantary Hotel

MAP T1 ▪ 168 Moo 1, Rojana Road, Ayutthaya ▪ 035 337 177 ▪ www. kantarycollection.com ▪ BB
This is the best choice for an overnight's stay in Ayutthaya. A great-value stylish hotel with ideal suites for families, it also has a swimming pool, Jacuzzi, and sauna.

Avani Hua Hin Resort and Villas

MAP S3 ▪ 1499 Phetkasem Road, Hua Hin ▪ 032 898 989 ▪ www. avanihotels.com ▪ BBB
Set around landscaped gardens and three expansive swimming pools, this chic hotel offers a variety of rooms – including pool villas and some with Jacuzzis on their balconies. There is also a contemporary spa and a fine Italian beachfront restaurant.

Hilton Hua Hin Resort & Spa

MAP S3 ▪ 33 Nares Damri Road, Hua Hin ▪ 032 538 999 ▪ www3. hilton.com ▪ BBB
There may be newer and more spectacular hotels in Hua Hin, but the Hilton is within walking distance of old Hua Hin and the Night Market. It also fronts onto a beautiful beach, and its top-floor restaurant is one of the best in town.

Novotel Suvarnabhumi Airport Hotel

MAP T2 ▪ Next to the airport terminal and SARL station ▪ 02 131 1111 ▪ www.novotel. com ▪ BBB
If an airport hotel is needed, this is by far the best. The rooms are very elegant, and there is an excellent spa. Enjoy a relaxing atmosphere, and good food at any of the five restaurants and cafés situated just off the atrium lobby.

Sugar Hut

MAP U3 ▪ 391/38 Moo 10, Pattaya Na Jomtien Road, Pattaya ▪ 038 251 686 ▪ www.sugar-hut. com ▪ BBB
Stay here for elegant Thai-style villas beyond the busy part of town, with superb gardens, Jacuzzi, a pool, and great Thai food.

For a key to hotel price categories see p114

General Index

Page numbers in **bold** refer to main entries.

A

Absolute monarchy 38
Accessories 27, 80
Accommodation 113, 114–17
Adhere the 13th 56, 74
Aerobics 62
Air travel 108, 109
Aisawan Thipphaya-at Pavilion (Bang Pa-In) 34
Alcohol 63
Amarin Winichai Hall 14
Amulet Market 70–71
Anantara Siam Spa 44
Angkor Wat, model of 12
Antiques 27
Aphonphimok Pavilion 15
Art, buying 27
Art galleries *see* Museums and galleries
Artist's House (Khlong Bang Luang) 62, 90
ASEAN Barred Ground Dove Festival (Yala) 65
Asiatique the Riverfront 6, 60
Assumption Cathedral 85, 87
L'Atelier de Joël Robuchon 58, 91
Ayutthaya 7, 11, **32–5**, 104
art from 16
hotels 117
overrun by Burmese 38
sights in and around 34–5
sleep-on-board cruise to 90
Ayutthaya Historical Study Center 32

B

Baats (alms bowls) 70
Baiyoke Tower II 88
Bamboo Bar 56, 93
Bamrung Muang Road 71, 72
Ban Khrua silk weavers 29
Bang Krajao 49, 90, 97
eco resort 117
Bang Pa-In 34, 103

Bangkok Art & Culture Centre 43, 62
Bangkok Butterfly Garden and Insectarium 51, 63
Bangkok Dolls Museum 51, 98
Banking 110, 111
Banyan Tree Spa 44
Bargaining 63
Bars, clubs and pubs 56–7
Downtown 92–3
Greater Bangkok 100–101
Old City 74
Beer 54, 63, 101
Beyond Bangkok 102–5
A Day and a Night in Pattaya 105
hotels 117
map 102
sights 103–5
Bhumibol Adulyadej *see* Rama IX
Bicycle travel 109
Blue Elephant 6, 58, 99
Boat noodles 24
Boats
canals 20
Damnoen Saduak Floating Market 25
sporting events 47
traveling by 108, 109
ways to enjoy the river 90
Bodhi tree 41
Bo.Lan 58, 99
Books 27
Borommaracha I, King 35
Borommaracha II, King 33, 35
Borommatrailokanat, King 33, 35
Bots 41
Wat Arun 31
Wat Pho 19
Wat Phra Kaeo **12–13**
Boutique hotels 116
Bowling 47
Boxing *see* Thai boxing
Brown Sugar: The Jazz Boutique 7, 57, 74
Buddha
images of 41
see also Golden Buddha; Reclining Buddhas

Buddhaisawan Chapel (National Museum) 16, 69, 73
Buddhism
spirits 70
see also Festivals; Temples, Buddhist
Budget travel 113, 116–17
Bunker, Chang and Eng 39
Bus travel 108, 109
Business hotels 115

C

Cabaret 6, 55, 101, 105
Cafés
Chinatown 81
Old City 75
Calypso Cabaret 6, 55, 60, 101
Canals 10, **20–21**
tours 70, 90
Car hire 109
Car travel 109
Carvings, Burmese 29
Cat Expo 65
Cell phones 63
Central Clock Tower (Chatuchak Weekend Market) 27
Central *prang* (Wat Arun) 30, 31
Central World 36–7, 60
Ceramics 80, 95
Chakri dynasty 38
Chakri Maha Prasat 14
Chan-ocha, General Prayut 39
Chantarakasem Palace Museum (Ayutthaya) 34
Chao Mae Tubtim Shrine 48, 88
Chao Phraya, General *see* Rama I
Chao Phraya Express 21, 90
Chao Phraya River 21
riverside restaurants (Tha Maharaj) 73
tours 70
ways to enjoy 90
Chao Sam Phraya National Museum 33
Charmchuri Art Gallery 43

Chatuchak 97
Chatuchak Park 26
Chatuchak Weekend
   Market 11, **26–7**, 95, 97
Chedis 41
   Phra Si Rattana Chedi
   (Wat Phra Kaeo) 12, 69
   Wat Pho 19
Chi, The Spa 44
Chiang Mai Cricket
   Sixes 47
Chiang Mai Flower
   Festival 65
Children's attractions
   50–51
Children's Discovery
   Museum 51
Chinatown 76–81
   Exploring Chinatown
   and Little India 79
   map 76–7
   restaurants and cafés 81
   sights 76–9
   what to buy 80
Chinese Guards (Wat
   Arun) 30
Chinese New Year 64
Chula-Thammasat
   Football Match 47
Chulalongkorn
   see Rama V
Chulalongkorn University
   88
Churches and cathedrals
   Assumption Cathedral
   85, 87
   Church of Santa Cruz 98
   Dusit district churches
   98
   St. Joseph's Cathedral
   (near Ayutthaya) 35
Cinema 49, 65
Climate 111
Clothing 27
The Club @ Koi 56, 93
Clubs see Bars, clubs a
   nd pubs
Conrad, Joseph 86
Corrections Museum 73
Country festivals 65
Coup d'état (1932) 38
Coup d'état (1992) 39
Coup d'état (2006) 39
Coup d'état (2014) 39
Crafts 26, 80, 112
Cricket 47
Cruises, river 90
Cultural shows 54–5, 101

Currency 110
Customs and Immigration
   110
Cycling 46, 47
   getting around 109

D
Dachanee, Tawan 42
Damnoen Saduak
   Floating Market 7, 11,
   24–5, 103
Dan Sai 65
Dance 54–5, 62
   festivals 64
"Death Railway" 104,
   105
Dining 113
Dinner cruises 90
Dinner shows 54, 55
Downtown 84–93
   A Walk through the Old
   Farang Quarter 87
   map 84–5
   restaurants 91
   shopping malls 89
   sights 85–8
   ways to enjoy the river
   90
Dream World 50
Durian fruit 97
Dusit Throne Hall 14
Dvaravati Buddha torso
   (Jim Thompson House)
   29
Dvaravati Wheel of Law
   (National Museum) 17

E
East Asiatic Company
   87
Eat Me 59, 91
Electrical appliances
   111
Elephant Round-Up
   (Surin) 65
Emerald Buddha 12, 15,
   69
Emergency Services 110,
   111
Emporium 61, 89
EmQuartier 61, 89
EmQuartier Tropical 48
Entertainment venues
   54–5, 101
Erawan Bangkok 89
Erawan National Park
   105
Erawan Shrine 62, 86

F
Farang Guards (Wat Pho)
   19
Festivals 47, 64–5
Floating vendors 20, 25
Floral Culture Museum
   49
Flow House 51
Flowers 80
Food and drink
   Chatuchak Weekend
   Market 27
   culinary highlights
   59
   Damnoen Saduak
   Floating Market 24
   malls 63
   where to eat 113
Football 47
Forts
   Mahakan Fort 73
   Phra Sumen Fort 72
Free attractions 62–3
French Embassy 87
Fruit 24, 97
Funarium 50

G
Gaggan 59, 91
Gardens see Parks and
   gardens
Gay bars and clubs 57
Gaysorn Plaza 89
General Post Office 87
Giant Swing (Wat Suthat)
   40, 71
Gold 78, 80
Golden Buddha (Wat
   Traimit) 40, 76, 79
Golden Mount 40, 70,
   71
Golf 46
Grand Palace 10, **14–15**,
   69, 82–3
   itineraries 6, 7
The Grande Spa 45
Greater Bangkok
   94–101
   bars and pubs 100
   Exploring Chauchak and
   Thonburi 97
   map 94–5
   nightclubs and
   entertainment 101
   restaurants 99
   sights 95–8
Gutis 41
   Wat Pho 19

H

H Gallery 7, 42
Haroon Mosque 87
Health 110, 111
Health Land 45
Hia Kui Market 24
Hinduism 70, 88
History 38–9
Ho trai 41
Home decor 26, 89
Hongsakula, Aspara 39
Hor Phra Monthein Tham
  (Wat Phra Kaeo) 13
Horse racing 46
Hostels 63
Hotels
  boutique 116
  budget 116–17
  business 115
  luxury 114–15
  mid-range 115–16
  rates and booking 113
Houses, traditional Thai
  20, 29, 43, 86
Hua Hin 104
  hotels 117
  Jazz Festival 65
Hua Lampong Station 79
Hyde and Seek 57

I

I. Sawan Residential Spa
  and Club 45
Ice skating 47
Incense 80
Inner Palace (Grand
  Palace) 14
Insurance 110
International Festival of
  Dance and Music 64
International Kite Festival
  47
Issaya Siamese Club 58,
  91
Itineraries
  A Day and a Night in
    Pattaya 105
  A Stroll through the Old
    City 71
  A Walk through the Old
    Farang Quarter 87
  Exploring Chauchak and
    Thonburi 97
  Exploring Chinatown
    and Little India 79
  Four Days in Bangkok
    6–7
  Two Days in Bangkok 6

J

Jataka Tales 28
Jim Thompson House 6,
  7, 11, **28–9**, 87
Jomtien Beach (Pattaya)
  105

K

Kamthieng House 96
Kanchanaburi 105
  hotels 117
Khao Phra Tamnak
  (Pattaya) 105
Khao San Road 72
Khao Yai 104
Khaosai Galaxy 39
Khlong Bangkok Noi 21
Khlong Bangkok Yai 21
Khlong Mon 20
Khon (masked theater) 43,
  54, 86
Khun Pitak Market 25
Kidzania 50
King Bhumibol's Birthday
  65
King Power Mahanakhon
  88
King Prajadhipok (Rama
  VII) Museum 72
King's Cup Regatta 47
Kinnaris (Wat Arun) 31
Kite-flying 47
Koh Kret 90, 95
Koh Samed 104
Koh Samui Regatta 47
Koh Si Chang 103
Kositpipat, Chalermchai
  39, 42
Kraprayoon, General
  Suchinda 39
Krisa Coffee Shop 71, 75
Kukrit Pramoj, Mom
  Rajawangse 39
  Heritage Home 89
Kwai, River 105

L

Lalai Sap Market 61
Laguna Phuket Triathalon
  47
Lak Muang 69, 70, 71
Lanna art 16
Lanna Boat Races 65
Lanterns 80
Leisure activities 46–7
Lenzi Tuscan Kitchen 58,
  91
Levels 57, 93

Little India 77
Liu 59, 91
Loha Prasat 72
Long-tail boats 90
Longboat races 47
Loy Krathong 65
Lumphini Boxing Stadium
  55, 101
Lumphini Park 46, 51,
  52–3, 63, 86
Luxury hotels 114–15

M

McIntyre, Thongchai 39
Magazines, listings 63,
  112
Maggie Choo's 56, 93
Mahakan Fort 73
Mahboonkrong Shopping
  Center (MBK) 60, 89
Mahidol *see* Rama VIII
Makha Puja 64
Malls 60–61, 63
Markets 60–61, 112
  Amulet Market 70–71
  Asiatique the Riverfront
    6, 60
  Chatuchak Weekend
    Market 11, **26–7**, 95,
    97
  Damnoen Saduak
    Floating Market 7, 11,
    24–5, 103
  floating 24, 106–7
  Hia Kui Market 24
  Khun Pitak Market 25
  Lalai Sap Market 61
  Pak Khlong Market 77,
    79
  Phahurat Market (Little
    India) 77
  Pratunam Market 88
  Sampeng Lane Market
    61
  Talad Kao 79
  Talad Mai 79
  Thewet Flower Market
    98
  Ton Kem Market 24
Martial arts 46
Massage
  traditional venues 63
  Wat Pho 10, 18, 73
  see also Spas
MBK Shopping Center 62
Media 111
Medicine Pavilion (Wat
  Pho) 18

Meditation (Wat Mahathat) 63, 72
Mini Siam (Pattaya) 105
Mon people 95
Mondops (Wat Arun) 31
Money-saving tips 63
Mongkut see Rama IV
Monks, Buddhist 41
  baats 70
  Wat Pho 19
Motorbike taxis 109
MRT 108, 109
Mount Krailas, model of 13
Muang Boran (Ancient City) 103
Muay Thai see Thai boxing
Murals
  temple 41
  Wat Phra Kaeo **12–13**, 69
  Wat Suthat 71
Museums and galleries 42–3
  The Art Center 43
  Bangkok Art & Culture Centre 43, 62
  Bangkok Dolls Museum 51, 98
  Chantarakasem Palace Museum (Ayutthaya) 34
  Chao Sam Phraya National Museum 33
  Children's Discovery Museum 51
  Corrections Museum 73
  Floral Culture Museum 49
  H Gallery 7, 42
  Jim Thompson House 6, 7, 11, **28–9**, 87
  Kamthieng House 96
  King Prajadhipok (Rama VII) Museum 72
  M.R. Kukrit's Heritage Home 87
  Museum of Contemporary Art 42
  Museum of Counterfeit Goods 88
  Museum of Forensic Medicine 49
  Museum of Siam 43, 72
  National Gallery 42, 72
  National Museum 6–7, 10, **16–17**, 42, 69
  Neilson Hays Library Art Galleries 63

Museums and galleries (cont.)
  Prasart Museum 98
  Queen Sirikit Museum of Textiles 6, 15, 48
  The Queen's Gallery 43
  Royal Barge Museum 7, 21, 42, 96, 97
  Silpakorn University Art Exhibition Hall 71, 73
  Suan Pakkad 43
  Wat Phra Kaeo Museum 15
Music 54–5
  Downtown venues 93
  festivals 64–5
  Greater Bangkok venues 101
Mythical creatures 13

N
Narai the Great, King 34, 35
Narai Phand 89
Naresuan, King 34, 35
National Gallery 42, 72
National Museum 6, 7, 10, **16–17**, 42, 69
National parks
  Erawan 105
  Khao Yai 104
National Theatre 54
Neilson Hays Library 63, 88
Newspapers 111
Nightlife 56–7
  Downtown 92–3
  Greater Bangkok 100–101
  Old City 74
  Pattaya 105
Nonthaburi 96
La Normandie 58, 91
Novices 41

O
The Oasis Spa 45
The Oasis Spa at Sukhumvit 51 44–5
Off the beaten path 48–9
Old City 68–75
  A Stroll through the Old City 71
  bars and clubs 74
  map 68
  restaurants 75
  sights 69–73

Opening hours 111
Orchards 24
Oriental Hotel 86, 87, 114
Oriental Spa 44

P
Pak Khlong Market 77, 79
Palaces
  Bang Pa-In (near Ayutthaya) 34
  Grand Palace 6–7, 10, **14–15**, 69, 82–3
  Phayathai Palace 96
  Wang Luang (Ayutthaya) 33
Pantip Plaza 61
Panyarachun, Anand 39
Parks and gardens
  Bang Krajao 49
  Chatuchak Park 26
  EmQuartier Tropical 48
  Jim Thompson House 28
  Lumphini Park 46, 51, 52–3, 63, 86
  Phra Athit Park 62
  Rama IX Royal Park 97
  Romaninart Park 73
  Sanam Luang 69
  Santichaiprakhan Park 73
  Saranrom Park 73
  Siwalai Gardens (Grand Palace) 15
  see also National parks; Theme parks
Passports 110, 111
Patpong 85
Pattaya 104–5
  A Day and a Night in Pattaya 105
  hotels 117
  Music Festival 65
Peninsula Plaza 89, 112, 113
Personal security 110, 111
Phahurat Market (Little India) 77
Phaisan Thaksin Hall 15
Pharmacies 110
Phaulkon, Constantine 35
Phayathai Palace 96
Phi Ta Khon 65
Phra Athit Park 62
Phra Mondop (Wat Phra Kaeo) 12
Phra Phetracha, King 35

Phra Si Rattana Chedi (Wat Phra Kaeo) 12, 69
Phra Sihing Buddha image (National Museum) 16
Phra Sumen Fort 72
Phuket Marathon 47
Phuket Vegetarian Festival 65
Phumintharacha, King 35
Pibilsonggram, Plaek 39
Pich, Sopheap 42
Plants 26
Police 110, 111
Portuguese Embassy 87
Postal services 111
Poy Sang Long 65
Prajadhipok see Rama VII
Prasart Museum 98
Prasat Thong, King 35, 103
Pratunam 60
Pratunam Market 88
Pubs see Bars, clubs and pubs
Puppet shows 62

Q

The Queen Saovabha Memorial Institute 50, 85
The Queen's Gallery 43
Queen Sirikit Museum of Textiles 6, 15, 48

R

Radio 111
Rail travel 108, 109
    construction of first railway 38
    Thailand-Burma Railway 104, 105
Rama I, King 12, 14, 17, 19, 38, 68
Rama I Road 6, 7
Rama II, King 95
Rama III, King 30, 96
Rama IV, King 12, 15, 34, 38, 40
Rama V, King 15, 17
    Koh Si Chang 103
    Wat Benjamabophit 40
Rama VII, King 14
Rama VIII, King 39
Rama IX, King 39, 65
Rama IX Royal Park 97
Rama X, King 39, 65
Ramakien murals (Wat Phra Kaeo) 12, 69

Ramathibodi I, King 33, 35
Ramathibodi II, King 35
Rang Mahal 59, 91
Ratchadamnoen Boxing Stadium 55
Rattanakosin art 16
Rattanakosin Island 69, 76
Reclining Buddhas 19
    Wat Lokaya Sutharam (Ayutthaya) 33
    Wat Pho 10, 18, 41, 69
    Wat Yai Chai Mongkol (near Ayutthaya) 34
Red House (National Museum) 16
Restaurants 58–9, 113
    Chinatown 81
    Downtown 91
    Greater Bangkok 99
    Old City 75
    Pattaya 105
    Sathorn Road, Sois 10–12 48
    Tha Maharaj riverside 73
River City Shopping Complex 87
Rocket Festival 65
Romaninart Park 73
Royal Bangkok Sports Club 46, 88
Royal Barge Museum 7, 21, 42, 96, 97
Royal Funeral Chariots Gallery (National Museum) 17
Royal India 79, 81
Royal Orchid Sheraton 87, 114
Royal Pantheon 12
Royal Ploughing Ceremony 13, 64
Rub Aroon 75, 97

S

S&P, Maharaj Pier 71, 75
Saen Saeb Canal 21, 29
Safety
    personal security 110, 111
    travel safety advice 110, 111
Sailing 47
St. Joseph's Cathedral (near Ayutthaya) 35
Sala Chalermkrung Royal Theatre 54
Sala Rim Naam 55
Sampeng Lane 78, 79, 80

Sampeng Lane Market 61
Sanam Chai 71
Sanam Luang 69, 71, 73
Sanctuary of Truth (Pattaya) 105
Santichaiprakhan Park 73
Sao Ching Cha (Wat Suthat) 40, 71
Saranrom Park 73
Sathorn Road, Sois 10–12 48
Saxophone 56, 93, 101
Scala Cinema 49
SEA LIFE Bangkok Ocean World 50, 88
Shinawatra, Thaksin 39
Shinawatra, Yingluck 39
Shopping 60–61, 112, 113
    Chinatown 80
    Downtown malls 89
Siam Center 89
Siam Discovery Center 89
Siam Niramit 6, 54, 101
Siam Paragon 7, 60, 63, 89
Siam Square 86
Silk 28, 29
Silom Village 54
Silpakorn University Art Exhibition Hall 71, 73
Sirikit, Queen 43
Siwalai Gardens (Grand Palace) 15
Six Red Snooker World Championship 47
Sky Bar 56, 92
Skytrain 108, 109
Snooker 46, 47
Soi Ban Baat 70, 71
Soi Nana (Chinatown) 48
Soi Thonglor 95
Somerset Maugham, William 86
Songkran 64
Songwat Road 77
Souvenirs 25, 80
Spas 7, 44–5, 114, 117
Spices 80
Spirit House (Jim Thompson House) 28
Spirits 70
Sport 46–7
    events 47
Sri Suriyen 16
Studio Lam 57
Suan Pakkad 86
Subway 108, 109
Sukhothai art 17
Surin 65

T

T'ai chi 63
Takraw 46
Taksin the Great, King 31, 38
Talad Kao 79
Talad Mai 79
Tawadang German Brewery 54, 101
Taxis 109
Tea 80
Telephones 63, 111
Television 111
Temples, Buddhist 40–41
  free entry 62
  mythical creatures 13
  offerings 80
  Rakhang 98
  Wat Arun 11, 20, **30–31**, 95, 97
  Wat Benjamabophit 40
  Wat Bowoniwet 40, 72
  Wat Chai Wattanaram (near Ayutthaya) 35
  Wat Ga Buang Kim 78
  Wat Hua Krabeu 48
  Wat Indrawiharn 98
  Wat Kalayanamit 98
  Wat Lokaya Sutharam (Ayutthaya) 33
  Wat Mahathat 40, 63, 71
  Wat Mangkon Kamalawat (Wat Leng Noi Yee) 78
  Wat Na Phra Mane (near Ayutthaya) 34
  Wat Phanan Cheong (near Ayutthaya) 34
  Wat Pho 10, **18–19**, 41, 69, 73
  Wat Phra Kaeo 10, **12–13**, 41, 69, 71
  Wat Phra Mahathat (Ayyutthaya) 32, 72
  Wat Phra Ram (Ayutthaya) 33
  Wat Phra Si Sanphet (Ayutthaya) 33
  Wat Phu Khao Thong (near Ayutthaya) 35
  Wat Prayun 98
  Wat Puthaisawan (near Ayutthaya) 35

Temples, Buddhist (cont.)
  Wat Ratchabophit 41, 72
  Wat Ratchaburana (Ayutthaya) 33
  Wat Ratchanadda 72
  Wat Saket 40, 65, 70, 71
  Wat Suthat 40, 71
  Wat Suwannaram 40, 98
  Wat Thammikarat (Ayutthaya) 32
  Wat Traimit 40, 76, 79
  Wat Yai Chai Mongkol (near Ayutthaya) 34
Temples, Hindu, Maha Uma Devi Temple 88
Tennis 46
Terminal 21 61
Textiles 80
Tha Maharaj 6, 7, 73
Tha Saphan Taksin 6
Thai Boxing 47, 55, 62, 101
Thai Rak Thai party 39
Thailand Cultural Centre 55
Thammasat University 73
Theater 54–5
Theme parks
  Dream World 50
  Mini Siam (Pattaya) 105
  Muang Boran (Ancient City) 103
Thewet Flower Market 98
Thompson, Jim **28–9**
Thonburi 6, 97
Tickets, transport 109
Time difference 111
Tinsulanonda, Prem 39
Ton Kem Market 24
Tour of Thailand 47
Tourist information 112
Traffic 87
Transvestite cabaret (lady-boys) 55, 101, 104, 105
Travel 108–9
  money-saving tips 63
  safety advice 110, 111
Travelers with Specific Needs 110, 111
Treasure Spa 45
Trips and tours 112
  see also Itineraries
Tuk-tuks 109

V

Vajiralongkorn *see* Rama X
VAT refunds 63
Visakha Puja 64
Visas 110, 111

W

Walking 109
Wang Luang (Ayutthaya) 33
Wat *see* Temples, Buddhist
Wat Arun 11, 20, **30–31**, 95
  itineraries 6, 7, 97
Wat Pho 10, **18–19**, 41, 69, 73
  itineraries 6, 7
  Scripture Hall 22–3
Wat Phra Kaeo 10, **12–13**, 41, 69
  demon guard 82–3
  itineraries 6, 7, 71
Wat Phra Kaeo Museum 15
Wat Saket Fair 65
Water taxis 90
Weather 112
Wihans 41
  Wat Suthat 71
  Wihan Phra Mongkhon Bophit (Ayutthaya) 32
  Wihan Yot (Wat Phra Kaeo) 12
Wildlife
  Bangkok Butterfly Garden and Insectarium 51, 63
  Elephant Round-Up (Surin) 65
  endangered species 27
  The Queen Saovabha Memorial Institute 50, 85
  SEA LIFE Bangkok Ocean World 50, 88
World War II 104, 105

Y

Yaowarat Road 77, 78, 79, 80

Acknowledgments

Author
Ron Emmons is a Thailand-based British writer and photographer whose work has appeared in a wide variety of international magazines and guidebooks, including the *DK Eyewitness Travel Guide to Malaysia and Singapore*.

Additional contributor
Peter Holmshaw

Publishing Director Georgina Dee

Publisher Vivien Antwi

Design Director Phil Ormerod

Editorial Sophie Adam, Ankita Awasthi Tröger, Avanika, Michelle Crane, Rachel Fox, Lucy Richards, Sally Schafer, Sands Publishing Solutions

Cover Design Maxine Pedliham, Vinita Venugopal

Design Tessa Bindloss, Sunita Gahir, Bharti Karakoti, Rahul Kumar

Picture Research Susie Peachey, Ellen Root, Lucy Sienkowska, Oran Tarjan

Cartography Jasneet Kaur, Zafar ul Islam Khan, Suresh Kumar, James Macdonald, Reetu Pandey

DTP Jason Little

Production Poppy Werder-Harris

Factchecker Paul Gray

Proofreader Leena Lane

Indexer Helen Peters

Revisions Stuti Tiwari Bhatia, Shikha Kulkarni, Arushi Mathur, Bandana Paul, Anuroop Sanwalia, Priyanka Thakur, Azeem Siddiqui

Commissioned Photography David Henley, Alex Robinson, Rough Guides / Martin Richardson

Picture Credits

The publisher would like to thank the following for their kind permission to reproduce their photographs:

Key: a-above; b-below/bottom; c-centre; f-far; l-left; r-right; t-top

123RF.com: Pisanu Kusonsaratool 46–7, Wichit Sawatdee 73cla, Mr. Rapisan Swangphon 88br, Seksan Wasuwat 96clb

Alamy Stock Photo: age fotostock / Dave Stamboulis 56tl; Paul Brown 57tr; Chronicle 38tr; Thomas Cockrem 86ca; third cross 11cra; Dinodia Photos RM 50cb; Giulio Ercolani 96t; EyeEm Mobile GmbH / Wanwisa Hernandez 63c; Kevin Foy 61crb; Peter Horree 80clb; imageBROKER / Dirk Bleyer 20-1, / Josef Beck 79bl, / Mara Brandl 60tl; John Kellerman 63tl, 73crb, 88ca; Mike Lawrance 70tr; Pakorn Lopattanakij 105bl; William Manning 33c; mediacolor's 15tr; Christian Müller 103cra; Peter Adams Photography Ltd 4t; Massimo Piacentino 4clb; Pictorial Press Ltd 39tr; Igor Prahin 43t; Prisma Bildagentur AG / Raga Jose Fuste 4b; Sergi Reboredo 58cb; Simon Reddy 62br; Mervyn Rees 27tl; robertharding / Luca Tettoni 17cla; 69cr; Leonid Serebrennikov 86b; Dave Stamboulis 74tl; Rick Strange 35bl; Nunnicha Supagrit 95crb; Peter Treanor 54cb; Fabrizio Troiani 22–3; Ian Watt 102tl; ZUMA Press; Inc. 65cl.

Anantara Bangkok Riverside Resort & Spa: 90clb.

Baan Khanitha: 99cra.

Bangkok Marriott Hotel Sukhumvit: 100cl.

Banyan Tree Bangkok: 92bl.

Bridgeman Images: Luca Tettoni 6tr, 16c.

Calypso Cabaret: Dorling Kindersley / Alex Robinson 55bl, 101t.

Depositphotos Inc: tampatra@hotmail.com 14-5c.

Doll Museum, Bangkok: Dorling Kindersley / Alex Robinson 51cla.

Dreamstime.com: Aaa187 35cra; Ammcranfield 22cr; Assoonas 4cl; Atosan 7tr; Nontawat Boonmun 59tr; Carloscastilla 51tr; Kanjanee Chaisin 46tl; Jaromír Chalabala 3tr, 106-7; Chaopavit 13tl; Sakkarin Chinsoi 43br; Chirawan 10bl; Pitchathorn Chitnelawong 40cla; Cowardlion 7br, 21tr, 31tl; Daagron 4cla; Ionut David 26cla; Oleg Doroshenko 41br; Finallast 41tl; Santiago Rodríguez Fontoba 12bl; Gnomeandi 11bc; Gow927 50t; Simon Hack 4cr; Jorg Hackemann 2tr, 18bc, 36–7, 87tr; Nasrul Hudayah 54t; Ifocus 62cla; Iphotothailand 2tl, 8-9; Lukasz Janyst 32cla; Boonchoo Kaewyai 72bl; Khellon 80ca; Olga Khoroshunova 32crb, 33br; Teerasak Khunrach 49b; Hathaichanok Losunthonchai 21cr; Mai9111 22clb; Aliaksandr Mazurkevich 22-3; Mhoohao 71cl; Pranodh Mongkolthavorn 3tl, 66-7; Moori 10ca; Luciano Mortula 77tr; Chatchawan Narakornpijit 32-3; Nicousnake 18cla, 34bl; Ongchangwei 11cb; Outcast85 104-5; Sean Pavone 4crb; Anton Petrus 6cl; Dmitry Pichugin 103b; Apichat Pimsoda 33tc; Thanapat Pirmphol 60b; Pixattitude 30c; Pixs4u 21br; Presse750 47tr; Sakol Promla 32–3; Psstockfoto 96-7; RIRFStock 19tl; Saiko3p 14br, 22cla, 23cla, 32cra; Melissa Schalke 11tl; Lee Snider 33tl; Nataliia Sokolovska 20bl; Maposee Soleh 34tr; Chatchai Somwat 47cl; Srckomkrit 10cb; StrippedPixel 76cl; Svglass 10br; Syda Productions 5tr; Tang90246 28cla; Tea 63br; Thaifairs 41cb; Tofudevil 19br; Tonfon 28br; Toxawww 27crb; Vladmax 85tr; Tawatchai

Wanasri 42ca; Boaz Yunior Wibowo 69b; Wichits 12cl; Sirawut Wisutipaitoon 33crb; Noppasin Wongchum 10cl; Richard Van Der Woude 82-3; Minyun Zhou 26br.

Gaggan: 59bl.

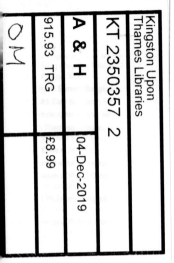

Penguin
Random
House

Printed and bound in China

First edition in 2008

Published in Great Britain
by Dorling Kindersley Limited
80 Strand, London WC2R 0RL

Published in the United States by
DK Publishing, 1450 Broadway, Suite 801,
New York, NY 10018, USA

Copyright © 2008, 2019 Dorling
Kindersley Limited

A Penguin Random House Company

19 20 21 22 10 9 8 7 6 5 4 3 2 1

**Reprinted with revisions 2010, 2012,
2014, 2017, 2019**

ISSN 1479-344X

ISBN 978-0-2413-6804-6

Cover

Front and spine: **Getty Images:** Seng Chye Teo.

Back: **Dreamstime.com:** Sean Pavone cla,
Korn Vitthayanukarun tl; **Getty Images:** Seng
Chye Teo; **iStockphoto.com:** kitchakron crb,
Yotsaran tr.

Pull Out Map Cover
Getty Images: Seng Chye Teo.

All other images © Dorling Kindersley
For further information see:
www.dkimages.com

*As a guide to abbreviations in visitor information
blocks:* **Adm** = admission charge; **D** = dinner;
L = lunch.

MIX
Paper from
responsible sources
FSC™ C018179

SPECIAL EDITIONS OF DK TRAVEL GUIDES

DK Travel Guides can be purchased
in bulk quantities at discounted
prices for use in promotions or as
premiums. We also offer special
editions and personalized jackets,
corporate imprints, and excerpts
from all our books, tailored
specifically to meet your needs.

To find out more, please contact:

in the US
specialsales@dk.com

in the UK
travelguides@uk.dk.com

in Canada
specialmarkets@dk.com

in Australia
penguincorporatesales@
penguinrandomhouse.com.au

Phrase Book

Thai is a tonal language and regarded by most linguists as head of a distinct language group, though it incorporates many Sanskrit words from ancient India, and some of modern English ones, too. There are five tones: mid, high, low, rising, and falling. The particular tone, or pitch, at which each syllable is pronounced determines its meaning. For instance "mãi" (falling tone) means "not," but "mãi" (rising tone) is "silk." In the second column of this phrase book is a phonetic transliteration of the Thai script for English speakers, including guidance for tones in the form of accents. In polite speech, Thai men add **"krúp"** at the end of each sentence; women add **"kã"** at the end of questions and **"kã"** at the end of statements.

Guidelines for Pronunciation

When reading the phonetics, pronounce syllables as if they form English words. For instance:

a	as in "ago"
e	as in "hen"
i	as in "thin"
o	as in "on"
u	as in "gun"
ah	as in "rather"
ai	as in "Thai"
air	as in "pair"
ao	as in "Mao Zedong"
ay	as in "day"
er	as in "enter"
ew	as in "few"
oh	as in "go"
oo	as in "boot"
OO	as in "book"
oy	as in "toy"
g	as in "give"
ng	as in "sing"

These sounds have no close equivalents in English:

eu	can be likened to a sound of disgust - the sound could be written as "errgh"
bp	a single sound between a "b" and a "p"
dt	a single sound between a "d" and a "t"

Note that when "p," "t," and "k" occur at the end of Thai words, the sound is "swallowed." Also note that many Thais use an "l" instead of an "r" sound

The Five Tones

Accents indicate the tone of each syllable.

no mark	The **mid tone** is voiced at the speaker's normal, even pitch.
á é í ó ú	The **high tone** is pitched slightly higher than the mid tone.
à è ì ò ù	The **low tone** is pitched slightly lower than the mid tone.
ã ẽ ĩ õ ũ	The **rising tone** sounds like a questioning pitch, starting low and rising.
â ê î ô û	The falling tone sounds similar to an syllable word for emphasis.

In an Emergency

Help!	chôo-ay dóo-ay!
Fire!	fai mâi!
Where is the nearest hospital?	tãir-o-née mee rohng pa-yah-bahn yòo têe-nãi?
Call an ambulance!	rêe-uk rót pa-yah-bahn hãi nòy!
Call a doctor!	rêe-uk mõr hãi nòy!
Call the police!	rêe-uk dtum ròo-ut hãi nòy!

Communication Essentials

Yes	châi or krúp/kã
No	mâi châi or mâi krúp/mâi kã
Please can you…?	chôo-ay
Thank you	kòrp-kOOn
No, thank you	mâi ao kòrp-kOOn
Excuse me/sorry	kôr-tôht (krúp/kã)
Hello	sa-wùt dee (krúp/kã)
Goodbye	lah gòrn ná
What?	a-rai?
Why?	tum-mai?
Where?	têe nãi?
How?	yung ngai?

Useful Phrases

How are you?	kOOn sa-bai dee reu (krúp/kã)?
Very well, thank you	sa-bai dee (krúp/kã)
How do I get to…?	…bpai yung-ngai?
Do you speak English?	kOOn pôot pah-sãh ung-grìt bpen mái?
Could you speak slowly?	chôo-ay pôot cháh cháh nòy dâi mái?
I can't speak Thai.	pôot pah-sãh tai mâi bpen

Useful Words

hot	rórn
cold	yen or não
good	dee
bad	mâi dee
enough	por
open	bpèrt
closed	bpìt
left	sái
right	kwãh
near	glâi
far	glai
straight ahead	yòo dtrong náh
woman/women	pôo-yĩng
man/men	pôo-chai
child/children	dèk
entrance	tahng kâo
exit	tahng òrk
toilet	hõrng náhm

Keeping in Touch

Where is the nearest public telephone?	tãir-o née mee toh-ra-sùp yòo têe-nãi?
Can I call abroad from here?	ja toh bpai dtàhng bpra-tâyt jàhk têe née dâi mái?
Hello, this is… speaking.	hello (põm /dee-chún)…pôot (krúp/kã)
May I leave a message?	kõr fàhk sùng a-rai nòy dâi mái?
I would like to speak to…	kõr pôot gùp khun… nòy (krúp/kã)
local call	toh-ra-sùp pai nai tórng tìn
phone card	but toh-ra-sùp

Shopping

How much does this cost?	nêe rah-kah tâo-rài?
I would like…	dtôrng-gahn…
Do you have?	mee… mái?
I am just looking	chom doo tâo-nún
Do you take credit cards/travelers' checks?	rúb but cray-dìt/ chék dern tang mái?
What time do you open/close?	bpèrt/bpìt gèe mohng?
Can you ship this overseas?	sóng khŏng nee bpai dtähng bpra-tâyt dâi mái?
Could you lower the price a bit?	lót rah-kah nòy dâi mái?
How about…baht?	…bàht dâi mái?
That's a little expensive.	pairng bpai nòy
Will you go for… baht?	…bàht bpai mái?
I'll settle for… baht.	…bàht gôr láir-o-gun
cheap	tòok
expensive	pairng
Does it come in other colors?	mee sĕe èun èek mái?
black	sĕe dum
blue	sĕe núm ngern
green	sĕe kĕe-o
red	sĕe dairng
white	sĕe kăo
yellow	sĕe lĕu-ung
gold	torng
silver	ngern
Thai silk	pâh-măi tai
ladies' wear	sêu-pâh sa-dtree
bookstore	ráhn kăi núng-sĕu
department store	hâhng
pharmacy	ráhn kăi yah
market	dta-làht
newsstand	ráhn kăi núng-sĕu pim
shoe shop	ráhn kăi rorng táo
supermarket	sÓOp-bpêr-mah-gèt
tailor	ráhn dtùt sêu-a

Staying in a Hotel

Do you have a vacant room?	mee hôrng wâhng mái?
air-conditioned room	hôrng air
I have a reservation.	jorng hôrng wái láir-o
I'd like a room for one night/three nights.	(pŏm/dee-chún) ja púk yòo keun nèung/ săhm keun
What is the charge per night?	kâh hôrng wun la tâo-rài?
I don't know yet how long I'll stay	măi sâhp wâh ja yòo nahn tâo-rài
May I see the room first please?	kŏr doo hôrng gòrn dâi mái?
May I leave some things in the safe?	kŏr fàhk kŏrng wái nai dtôo sáyf dâi mái?
Will you spray some mosquito repellent, please?	chôo-ay chèet yah gun yOOng hâi nòy dâi mái?
double/twin room	hôrng kôo
single room	hôrng dèe-o
bedroom	hôrng norn
bill	bin
fan	pùt lom
hotel	rohng-rairm
key	gOOn-jair
manager	pôo-jùt-gahn
mosquito screen	mÚÖng lôo-ut
shower	fùk boo-a
swimming pool	sá wâi náhm

Sightseeing

travel agent	bor-ri-sùt num têe-o
tourist office	sŭm-núk ngahn gahn tôrng têe-o
tourist police	dtum-ròo-ut tôrng têe-o
beach	hàht or chai-hàht
cliff	nâh pàh
festival	ngahn órk ráhn
hill/mountain	kăo
historical park	ÒO-ta-yahn-bpra wùt sàht
island (koh)	gòr
lake	ta-lay sáhp
museum	pí-pít-ta-pun
national park	ÒO-ta-yahn hàirng châht
palace	wang
park/garden	sŏo-un
river	mâir náhm
ruins	boh-rahn sa-tăhn
temple (wat)	wút
Thai boxing	moo-ay tai
Thai massage	nôo-ut
trekking	gahn dern tahng táo
waterfall	náhm dtòk
zoo	sŏo-un sàt

Transportation

When does the train for…leave?	rót fai bpai…òrk meu-rài?
How long does it take to get to…?	chái way-lah nahn tâo-rài bpai tĕung têe…?
A ticket to… please.	kŏr dtŏo-a bpai… nòy (krúp/kâ)
Which platform for the… train?	rót fai bpai… yòo chahn cha-lah năi?
What station is this?	têe nêe sa-tăhn-nee a-rai?
I'd like to reserve a seat, please.	kŏr jorng têe nûng
Where is the bus station?	sa-tăhn-nee rót may yòo têe-năi?
Which buses go to…?	rót may sài năi bpai…?
What times does the bus for… leave?	rót may bpai… òrk gèe mohng?
Would you tell me when we get to… ?	tĕung… láir-o chôo-ay bòrk dôo-ay?
Is it far?	glai mái?
ticket	dtŏo-a
air-conditioned bus	rót bprùp ah-gàht
airport	sa-năhm bin
tour bus	rót too-a
train	rót fai
bus station	sa-tăhn-nee rót may
moped	rót mor-dter-sai
bicycle	rót jùk-gra-yahn
taxi	táirk-sêe

Eating Out

A table for two please.	kŏr dtó sŭm-rùp sŏrng kon

May I see the menu?	kŏr doo may-noo nòy?
Do you have… ?	mee… mái?
I'd like…	kŏr…
I didn't order this.	nêe mâi dâi sùng (krúp/kà)
Is it spicy?	pèt mái?
Not too spicy, ok?	mâi ao pèt mâhk na
I can eat Thai food.	tahn ah-hăhn tai bpen
May I have a glass of water, please.	kŏr núm kăirng bplào gâir-o nèung
Waiter/waitress!	kOOn (krúp/kà)
The check, please.	kŏr bin nòy (krúp/kà)
bottle	kòo-ut
chopsticks	dta-gée-up
drink(s)	krêu-ung dèum
fork	sôrm
glass	gâir o
menu	may-noo
spoon	chórn

Menu Decoder

nòr mái	bamboo shoots
glôoy-ay	banana
néu-a woo-a	beef
bee-a	beer
dtôm	boiled
yâhng	char-grilled
gài	chicken
prík	chili
gah-fair	coffee
bpoo	crab
mèe gròrp	crispy noodles
gŏo-ay dtěe-o hâirng	dry noodles
bpèt	duck
tÓO-ree-un	durian
kài	egg
bplah	fish
king	ginger
núm kăirng bplào	iced water
ka-nŎOn	jackfruit
mâir-kŏhng	Mekong Whisky
hèt	mushroom
gŏo-ay dtěe-o-náhm	noodle soup
ma-la-gor	papaya
sùp-bpa-rót	pineapple
néu-a-mŏo	pork
kâo	rice
gŏo-ay dtěe-o	rice noodles
gÔOng	shrimp
núm see éw	soup
ah-hăhn wähng	soy sauce
pùk ka-náh	spring greens
kâo-něe-o	sticky rice
kâo pôht	sweet corn
núm chah	tea
pùk	vegetables
náhm	water

Health

I do not feel well	róâ-sèuk mâi sa-bai
It hurts here.	jèp dtrong née
I have a fever.	dtoo-a-rórm bpen kâi
sore throat	jèp kor
stomach ache	bpòo-ut tórng
vomit	ah-jee-un
asthma	rôhk hèut
cough	ai
diabetes	rôhk bao wähn

diarrhea	tórng sěe-a
dizzy	wee-un hŏo-a
dysentery	rôhk bit
fever	kâi
headache	bpòo-ut hŏo-a
aspirin	air-sa-bprin or yah-gâir kâi
doctor	mŏr
dentist	tun-dta-pâirt or mŏr fun
hospital	rohng pa-yah-bahn
injection	chèet yah
medicine	yah
prescription	bai sùng yah
How many tablets do I take?	dtôrng gin yah gèe mét dtòr krúng
I'm allergic to…	(pŏm/dee-chún) páir…

Numbers

0	sŏon
1	nèung
2	sŏrng
3	săhm
4	sèe
5	hâh
6	hòk
7	jèt
8	bpàirt
9	gâo
10	sìp
11	sìp-èt
12	sìp-sŏrng
13	sìp-săhm
14	sìp-sèe
15	sìp-hâh
16	sìp-hòk
17	sìp-jét
18	sìp-bpàirt
19	sìp-gâo
20	yêe-sìp
30	săhm-sìp
40	sèe-sìp
50	hâh-sìp
60	hòk-sìp
70	jèt-sìp
80	bpàirt-sìp
90	gâo-sìp
100	nèung róy
1,000	nèung pun
10,000	nèung mèun
100,000	nèung săirn

Time

one minute	nèung nah-tee
one hour	nèung chôo-a mohng
half an hour	krêung chôo-a mohng
Sunday	wun ah-tít
Monday	wun jun
Tuesday	wun ung-kahn
Wednesday	wun pÓOt
Thursday	wun pa-réu-hùt
Friday	wun sÒOk
Saturday	wun sǎo
a day	neung wun
a week	nèung ah-tít
a weekend	sÒOt sùp-pah-dah
a month	nèung deu-un
a year	nèung bpee